# WORLD OF WoW WONDER

# THE REALLY BIG AWESOME Book

### ALL ABOUT FLESH-EATERS, GIANT PLANT-EATERS, DUCKBILLS, BONEHEADS, & ARMORED DINOSAURS

Get ready to hear your kids say, "Wow! That's awesome!" as they dive into this fun, informative, question-answering book! Students—and teachers and parents—will learn things about the prehistoric world that they never knew before!

This approach to education seeks to promote an interest in learning by answering questions kids have always wondered about. When books answer questions that kids already want to know the answers to, kids love to read those books, fostering a love for reading and learning, the true keys to lifelong education.

Colorful graphics are labeled and explained to connect with visual learners, while entertaining explanations of each subject will connect with those who prefer reading or listening as their learning style.

This educational book makes learning fun through many levels of interaction. The in-depth information combined with fantastic illustrations promote learning and retention, while question and answer boxes reinforce the subject matter to promote higher order thinking.

Teachers and parents love this book because it engages young people, sparking an interest and desire in learning. It doesn't feel like work to learn about a new subject with a book this interactive and interesting.

This book will be an addition to your home or classroom library that everyone will enjoy. And, before you know it, you too will be saying, "Wow! That's awesome!"

*"People cannot learn by having information pressed into their brains. Knowledge has to be sucked into the brain, not pushed in. First, one must create a state of mind that craves knowledge, interest, and wonder. You can teach only by creating an urge to know."*
*- Victor Weisskopf*

## WORLD OF DINOSAURS 6

## FLESH-EATERS 18

## GIANT PLANT-EATERS 44

# DUCKBILLS AND BONEHEADS 70

# ARMORED DINOSAURS 96

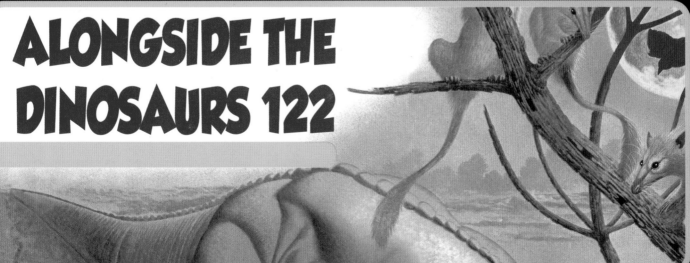

# ALONGSIDE THE DINOSAURS 122

PRESERVED

8

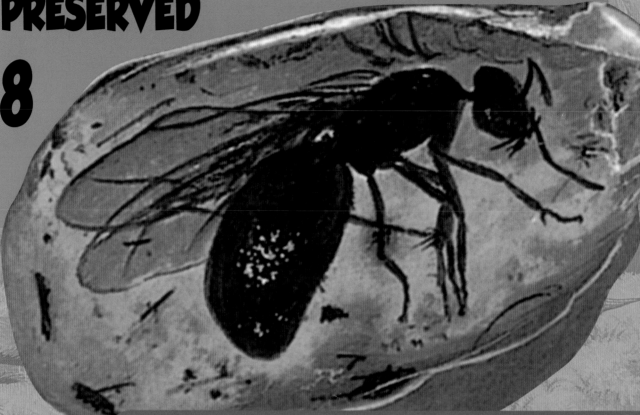

WHEN THEY LIVED 10

DIGGING THEM UP 12

# DINOSAUR GROUPS 16

# FIRST PREHISTORIC CREATURES 14

# THE WORLD OF DINOSAURS

Dinosaurs were among the most successful animals of all time. They lived on Earth for over 160 million years, and they were big. Some were very big indeed. Scientists called "paleontologists" study remains that have been preserved in ancient rocks. They have unearthed amazing information and are constantly making exciting new discoveries about dinosaurs.

This insect has been preserved in amber.

Mososaurus

Carnotaurus

Euoplocephalus

## Awesome facts

In the film *Jurassic Park*, scientists used bits of DNA (genes) preserved in fossils to bring dinosaurs back to life. We know, however, that this is impossible.

Pteranodon

Tarbosaurus

Lambeosaurus

Baryonyx

**Q: What are dinosaur remains called?**

**A:** The bones, shells, leaves, and other remains that have been preserved in rock are called "fossils." Fossils of dinosaurs, and of plants and animals that lived with them, have been found all over the world.

Styracosaurus

Albertosaurus

# WHEN THEY LIVED

Dinosaurs lived between 230 and 65 million years ago (mya). This is a very long time ago. It's hard enough to imagine hundreds of years ago, let alone millions. Dinosaurs are dated according to the geological time scale, which is used to age rocks. Scientists called "geologists" figure out the ages of ancient rocks by studying radioactive elements in them, and by analyzing fossils.

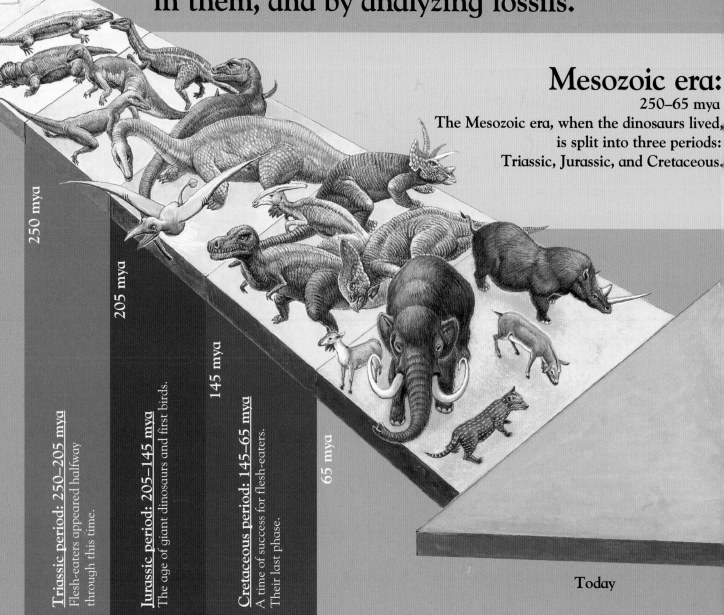

### Mesozoic era:
250–65 mya
The Mesozoic era, when the dinosaurs lived, is split into three periods: Triassic, Jurassic, and Cretaceous.

250 mya

205 mya

145 mya

65 mya

**Triassic period: 250–205 mya**
Flesh-eaters appeared halfway through this time.

**Jurassic period: 205–145 mya**
The age of giant dinosaurs and first birds.

**Cretaceous period: 145–65 mya**
A time of success for flesh-eaters. Their last phase.

Today

At the start of the age of the dinosaurs, the continents were all joined together as one great supercontinent called "Pangaea." Over millions of years, the Atlantic Ocean opened up and Pangaea split apart. The continents drifted to their present positions. They are still moving about an inch (a few centimeters) each year.

Today

50 mya

100 mya

200 mya

Pangaea ——

Continental drift

Q: Why is the dinosaur age split into sections?

A: The Mesozoic era—the time on the geological scale when dinosaurs lived—is split into periods, based on the rocks and creatures around at the time. The Triassic period came first. Its name comes from the Latin for "three" (tri) because the period had three distinct parts. Many fossils from this time have been found in Germany. The Jurassic period is named after the Jura mountains in France, where rocks of this age are common. Cretaceous comes from the Greek for "chalk," (creta) a common rock from this period.

Triassic period: 250–205 mya

Jurassic period: 205–145 mya

Cretaceous period: 145–65 mya

# DIGGING THEM UP

Digging up dinosaurs is a long and difficult business. First, you have to find a skeleton, then get it out of the rock and bring it home. Then begins the slow process of cleaning it, while making sure it doesn't crumble into bits.

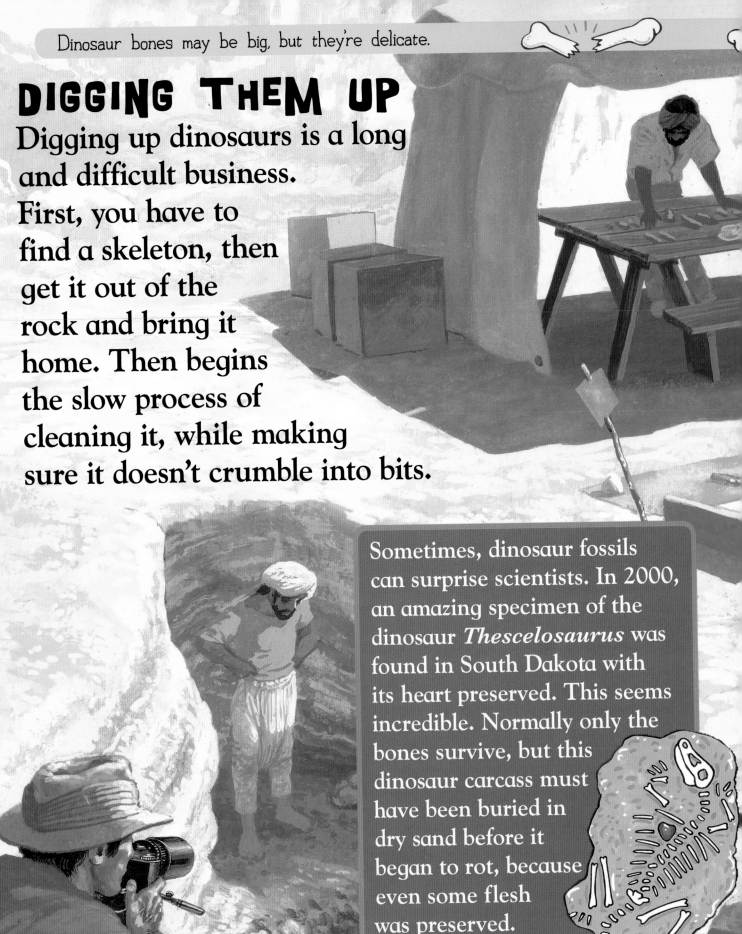

Sometimes, dinosaur fossils can surprise scientists. In 2000, an amazing specimen of the dinosaur *Thescelosaurus* was found in South Dakota with its heart preserved. This seems incredible. Normally only the bones survive, but this dinosaur carcass must have been buried in dry sand before it began to rot, because even some flesh was preserved.

**Q:** How did a flesh-eating dinosaur become a fossil?

**A:** Small meat-eating animals ate the flesh from the dead dinosaur's bones. Some bones rotted, but others were buried under layers of sand or mud. These turned into fossils over time, as tiny spaces in the bones filled with rock. Millions of years later, the fossilized bones are uncovered by water or wind action. Paleontologists dig the fossilized bones out of the rock and clean them, making sure they don't fall apart. They make maps and take photographs at the dig site so they know exactly where everything was found.

To protect fossilized dinosaur bones, strips of cloth are soaked in plaster and water, then wrapped around the bone in layers. As the plaster dries, it forms a tough protective shell.

# DINOSAUR EVOLUTION

Dinosaurs were not the first prehistoric creatures on Earth. The oldest fossils—very simple microbes—date back to an amazing 3,500 mya. The first sea animals appeared 600 mya, the first fish 500 mya, and the first reptiles 320 mya. The dinosaurs, also reptiles, evolved from these early reptiles. The first dinosaurs were found in rocks 230 million years old.

The first reptile survived on a diet of cockroaches, scorpions, and centipedes (above). It was called "*Hylonomus*," and lived in the great swamp forests of Canada 320 mya.

Up to 400 mya, there was not much life on land—just some small plants and bugs. Then, some unusual fish that could breathe with lungs as well as gills began to live on land for short periods. By 370 mya, one of these air-breathing fish had evolved legs. This was the first amphibian. Like modern frogs, these first amphibians still had to lay their eggs in water.

*Hylonomus*

# DINOSAUR GROUPS

There were five main groups of dinosaurs: the meat-eaters, called "theropods;" the big, long-necked plant-eaters, called "sauropodomorphs;" the armored plant-eaters, called "thyreophorans;" the horned dinosaurs, called "marginocephalians;" and the two-legged plant-eaters, called "ornithopods."

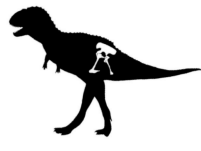

***Carnotaurus***
(Saurischia)

***Hypsilophodon***
(Ornithischia)

## Saurischia

| Theropoda | Sauropodomorpha |

*Eoraptor* lived 230 mya and was the world's first, most primitive dinosaur.

● ***Tyrannosaurus rex***

● ***Eoraptor***

All dinosaurs are classed into one of two subgroups, called the "saurischia" and the "ornithischia," according to the arrangement of their three hip bones (left). The saurischia, or "lizard hipped," had the three hip bones all pointing in different directions. The ornithischia, or "bird hipped," had both of the lower hip bones running backward.

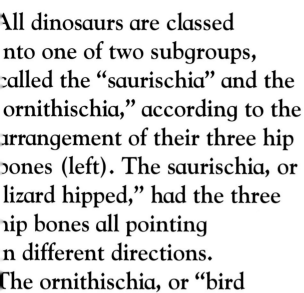

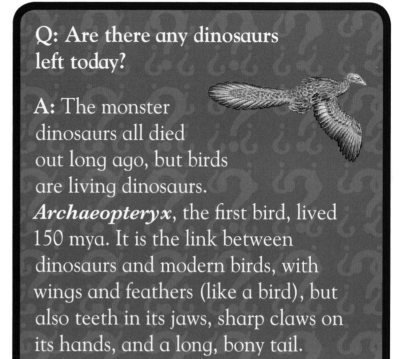

Q: Are there any dinosaurs left today?

A: The monster dinosaurs all died out long ago, but birds are living dinosaurs. *Archaeopteryx*, the first bird, lived 150 mya. It is the link between dinosaurs and modern birds, with wings and feathers (like a bird), but also teeth in its jaws, sharp claws on its hands, and a long, bony tail.

● *Apatosaurus*

| Thyreophora | Ornithischia | |
| | Marginocephalia | Ornithopoda |

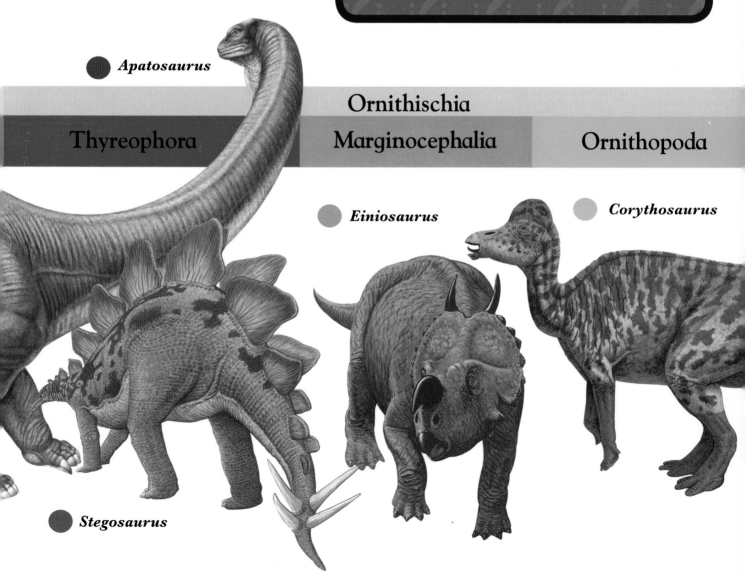

● *Einiosaurus*

● *Corythosaurus*

● *Stegosaurus*

TYRANNOSAURUS REX 20

SHARP CLAWS 22

THE FIRST FLESH-EATER 24

# WHAT'S IN A NAME

**28**

# TINY FLESH-EATERS 32

# HUGE FLESH-EATERS 40

# FLESH-EATERS

Flesh-eating dinosaurs, called "theropods," ranged from turkey-sized dinosaurs to the awesome *Tyrannosaurus rex*. Theropods of different sizes ate prey of different sizes. This meant that several species could live side-by-side.

*Ornithomimus*

In the Late Cretaceous period of Canada, smaller meat-eaters lived alongside the huge *T. rex*. *Troodon* hunted lizards, mammals, and even insects. It relied on speed and intelligence. *Ornithomimus* ate small plant-eating dinosaurs and the young of larger ones.

Big meat-eaters, like *T. rex*, ate the larger plant eaters. *T. rex* probably wasn't very fast or bright. It didn't need to be. It was so big, it could attack almost any other dinosaur.

*Troodon*

*T. rex* used its massive teeth to tear strips from its prey's flesh.

# WHAT MAKES A FLESH-EATER?

All flesh-eaters had sharp claws and sharp, curved teeth that pointed backwards. So if the prey struggled, it moved further into the gaping jaws. One of the most fearsome flesh-eaters was *Deinonychus.*

### Awesome facts

Most dinosaurs were not very smart, but Deinonychus had a big brain. It had to have a good sense of balance, excellent eyesight, and be able to communicate.

*Deinonychus*

Q: How did **Deinonychus** use its toe claw?

A: It had one huge claw on each foot, on the second toe. When running, it held the claw off the ground so it would not become blunt. But when it attacked, it raised its foot and slashed downwards, in a half circle.

*Deinonychus* was only as tall as a 10-year-old human, so it had to work in packs to bring down large prey like this *Tenontosaurus*.

*Tenontosaurus*

## BALANCING

Two-legged dinosaurs were like see-saws, balanced over their back legs. The front of the body had to weigh the same as the tail, or the dinosaur would fall on its nose. So flesh-eaters had to hold their backbones nearly flat when they ran, and flick their massive tails around to keep perfect balance.

# MAKING A MARK

The first flesh-eating dinosaur was *Herrerasaurus* from the Late Triassic period of Argentina, 230 mya. Medium-sized and good at hunting, *Herrerasaurus* liked to eat mammal-like reptiles called "cynodonts," which lived in burrows.

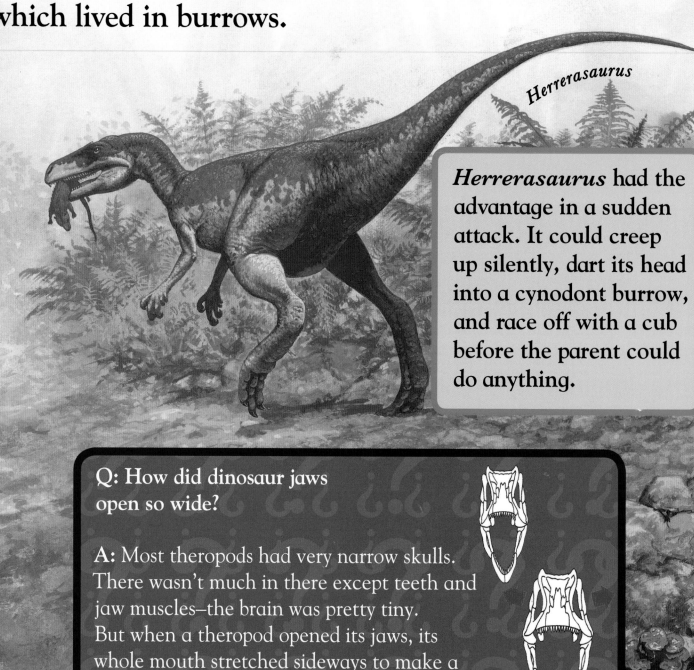

*Herrerasaurus*

*Herrerasaurus* had the advantage in a sudden attack. It could creep up silently, dart its head into a cynodont burrow, and race off with a cub before the parent could do anything.

Q: How did dinosaur jaws open so wide?

A: Most theropods had very narrow skulls. There wasn't much in there except teeth and jaw muscles—the brain was pretty tiny. But when a theropod opened its jaws, its whole mouth stretched sideways to make a bigger bite.

The ancestors of mammals belonged to the same mammal-like reptile group as cynodonts. Some cynodonts probably had hair and were warm-blooded. They could hunt at night, unlike the cold-blooded early dinosaurs.

Theropods all had powerful hands. Early ones, like *Herrerasaurus*, had four or five muscular fingers, each armed with a long, sharp claw. Later on, theropods usually had only three fingers, and some (like *T. rex*) had two.

Cynodont

## PREDATOR NUMBERS

Theropods were rarer than plant-eaters. This is because there must always be far fewer predators than prey animals, similar to lions and antelope today.

# HUNT TO THE DEATH

Fossilized footprints show that dinosaurs walked and swam in lakes. *Ceratosaurus* was the terror of North America 150 mya. But at 20 feet (6.1 meters) long, it took more than one *Ceratosaurus* to bring down the monster *Apatosaurus*, 69 feet (21 meters) long.

Q: Why did theropod skulls have so many holes?

A: Holes are lighter than bones, and a light skull can move faster. So flesh-eaters had thin bones with very big holes between them for its ears, eyes, nostrils, and jaw muscles.

*Ceratosaurus*

### Awesome facts

*Ceratosaurus* had horns on its head, in front of the eyes. These made it look more frightening and may have been used in fighting.

Small and medium-sized flesh-eaters like *Ceratosaurus* could clearly run fast and moved at 12-19 miles (19.3-30.6 kilometers) per hour. That's about the fastest you could sprint over a short distance. Bigger flesh-eaters may not have been able to sprint so fast, because they were so much heavier.

Albertosaurus

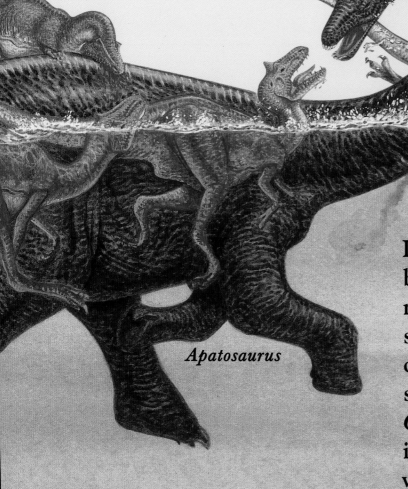

Apatosaurus

Pack hunting was risky business. *Apatosaurus* did not have powerful teeth or sharp claws, but it could whack out with its powerful tail and stun a predator. But if the *Ceratosaurus* kept biting into its flesh, the *Apatosaurus* would eventually become weak.

# WHAT'S IN A NAME?

The first dinosaurs were named nearly 200 years ago. Their names sometimes tell us something about the dinosaur itself. For example, *Ceratosaurus*, named in 1884, means "horned reptile," referring to the horns on its face.

Dilophosaurus

Megalosaurus

Yangchuanosaurus

Tuojiangosaurus

Muraenosaurus

Archaeopteryx

## Q: Who gave dinosaurs their names?

A: Dinosaurs are named by their discoverers. About 10 or 20 new species are still being named every year. If you find a new dinosaur skeleton that has never been named, you can make up a name and publish it!

Richard Owen made up the word "dinosaur" in 1842. It is Greek for "terrible lizard."

Othniel Marsh (above left) and Edward Cope (above right) named more dinosaurs than anyone else, between 1870 and 1900, including *Ceratosaurus*, *Allosaurus*, and *Stegosaurus*.

*Megalosaurus*, named in 1824, means "big reptile." This drawing shows what scientists then thought it looked like.

*Heterodontosaurus*

*Ceratosaurus*

# ALL OVER THE WORLD

Meat-eaters lived all over the world. *Allosaurus,* for example, is best known from the Late Jurassic period of North America, 150 mya, but remains have also been found in Tanzania in Africa, and possibly even in Australia.

The worldwide spread of *Allosaurus* is not surprising when you remember that the continents were joined together as the supercontinent Pangaea in the Jurassic period (see page 11). *Allosaurus* could have wandered from one end of the world to the other.

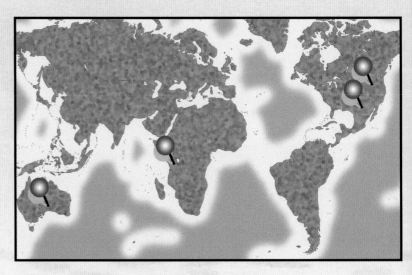

Sites of most *Allosaurus* finds.

## Awesome facts

The Australian *Allosaurus* find is not confirmed. It is in Early Cretaceous rocks, 50 million years younger than the other finds, and is only of part of a leg.

# SKULL HORNS

*Allosaurus*, like most meat-eaters, had knobs and lumps on its skull. What were they for? Maybe they just made its face look more scary. When rival *Allosaurus* males squared up to each other, the contender with the louder growl and bigger bumps would likely have been the winner.

Allosaurus

# TINY AND TERRIBLE

Some flesh-eaters were so tiny that a big plant-eating dinosaur like *Apatosaurus* would not even see them. But these midgets were pretty scary if you were a lizard or a rat-like mammal. Small size went with intelligence and speed.

*Compsognathus* lived in what is now Germany, and was the smallest dinosaur—a mere two feet (61 centimeters) long from its snout to the tip of its tail. One of the amazing fossils of this tiny hunter (right) even shows its last meal—a complete skeleton of the lizard *Bavarisaurus* inside its rib cage.

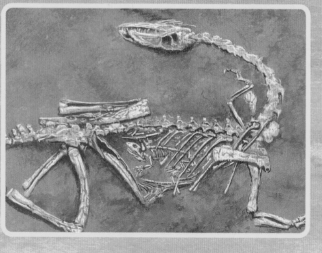

A small flock of *Compsognathus* are scattered (right) by a giant plant-eater. These little dinosaurs could move fast. They may even have had a fine covering of feathers over their bodies. They fed on lizards, frogs, and dragonflies.

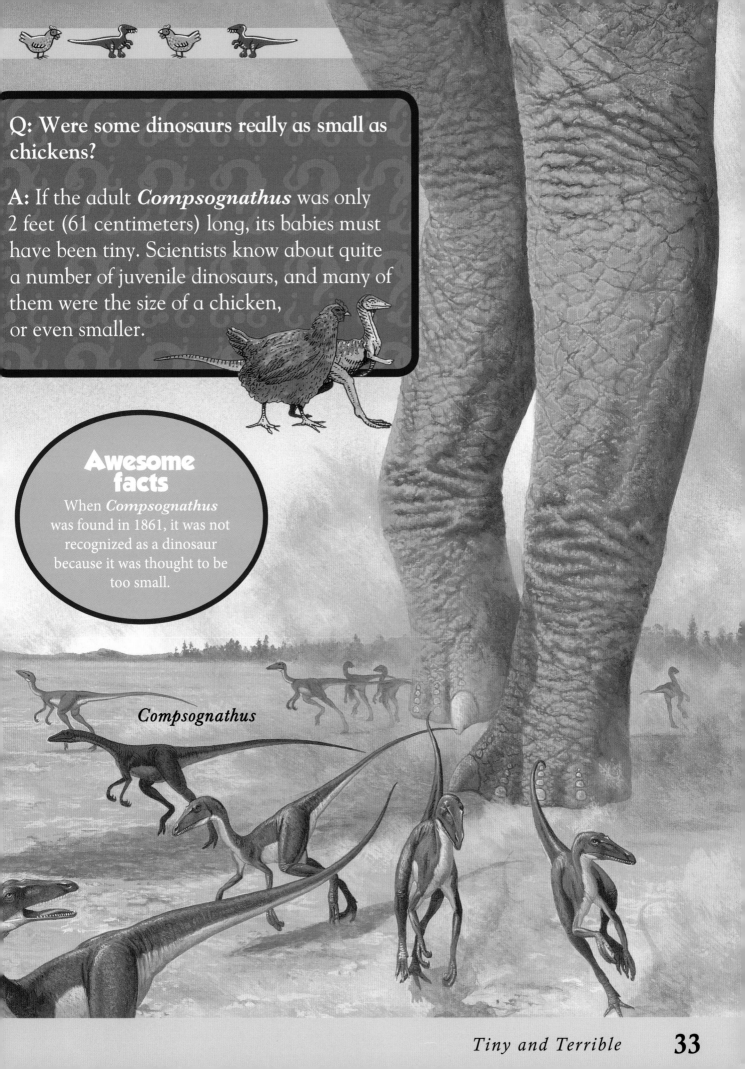

**Q: Were some dinosaurs really as small as chickens?**

**A:** If the adult *Compsognathus* was only 2 feet (61 centimeters) long, its babies must have been tiny. Scientists know about quite a number of juvenile dinosaurs, and many of them were the size of a chicken, or even smaller.

## Awesome facts

When *Compsognathus* was found in 1861, it was not recognized as a dinosaur because it was thought to be too small.

*Compsognathus*

New finds from China prove that many small theropods had feathers.

# FEATHERED FIND

Until the 1990s, feathers on dinosaurs was only a wild theory. Then, some startling finds in China proved that many small theropods had them. *Sinosauropteryx* and *Caudipteryx* are two of the new Chinese feathered dinosaurs, relatives of *Compsognathus.* Feathers on dinosaurs provide evidence that birds are living dinosaurs.

*Archaeopteryx* and *Compsognathus* were found in the same rocks in southern Germany. They were both named in 1861. Paleontologists soon noticed that the two skeletons were very similar and they suggested that dinosaurs had given rise to birds. This has been debated hotly for years, but it now seems clear that birds really are living theropod dinosaurs.

*Archaeopteryx*

Feathers are made from keratin, the same protein that makes up your nails and hair. Feathers are not often preserved as fossils, because they typically rot away before the carcass is buried. In some cases, if the feather is buried quickly, it will survive as a fossil.

## WINGS

A wing is just a fairly long arm that carries feathers. *Deinonychus* had long arms with strong hands, covered with short feathers. It is not hard to see how this could have evolved into a flying wing if the feathers grew longer.

*Deinonychus*

# FISHING CLAWS

Most theropods ate other dinosaurs or smaller land animals. One group, the spinosaurids, had crocodile-shaped skulls and may have been fish-eaters. Perhaps they used their strong hands to swipe fish out of the water, just as bears do today.

## Awesome facts

The spinosaurid *Baryonyx* from southern England was found by accident in 1983 by William Walker as he walked through his local brick works.

*Baryonyx*

Q: Why did spinosaurids have crocodile skulls?

A: The long, low snout and numerous teeth of the spinosaurids must have been ideal for holding struggling fish. Stronger jaws are needed only for larger prey. Spinosaurids looked far more like modern crocodiles than other theropods.

Spinosaurids had long spines on their vertebrae (backbone). These may have carried a thin covering of skin—a kind of sail, running along the backbone. Perhaps the sail was used in controlling body temperature—to take in heat when they were cold and to give off heat when they were overheated.

The spinosaurid *Baryonyx,* from the Early Cretaceous period of southern England, crouches silently beside a river and swipes out a fish with its long-clawed hand.

# NESTING

An astonishing find in 1995 in Mongolia showed that some meat-eaters sat on their eggs, just like modern birds, to protect them and keep them warm (or cool). Most modern reptiles lay their eggs then leave them.

*Oviraptor*

## DINOSAUR EGGS

Scientists dissect dinosaur eggs, and sometimes they find tiny bones inside. This tiny embryo lay curled up inside the eggshell—it must have died before it could hatch.

*Oviraptor* means "egg thief." It was named in 1924, and has had a bad reputation ever since. Paleontologists then thought this toothless theropod fed on eggs. But the reason it was found close to nests containing eggs was that it was a good parent, caring for its own young!

As good parents, dinosaurs probably helped to protect their young after they had hatched. They may have brought back food, partly chewed, to feed to their young. It might sound gross, but that's what many birds do.

# SIZING UP

The flesh-eating dinosaur *Tyrannosaurus rex*, from the Upper Cretaceous period of North America, was a monster. At 39 feet (11.9 meters) long and weighing up to 7.5 tons (6.8 metric tons), *T. rex* was truly awesome: It could swallow you in one gulp. But was it the biggest?

**Q: How big was a T. rex tooth?**

**A:** *T. rex* had teeth the size of steak knives. The tooth had two halves. The upper crown, which did the cutting business, was the size of a banana. The root, hidden in the jawbone, was just as big.

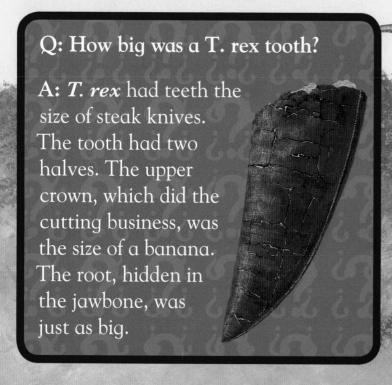

*T. rex*—terrifying hunter or humble scavenger? Some paleontologists think that *T. rex* was so massive that it could not have moved fast. It might have trundled about slowly, looking for rotting carcasses that had been killed by smaller, swifter theropods.

Other huge dinosaurs, such as *Carcharodontosaurus* from North Africa, and *Giganotosaurus* from Argentina, may have been longer than *T. rex*, but they were not as heavy.

## POOH!

In 2003, Canadian scientists found a giant dinosaur dropping, about 25 inches (63.5 centimeters) long, containing dinosaur bones. Whodunnit? *T. rex*, most likely.

# FLESH-EATERS' WORLD

From the tiny *Compsognathus* to the awesome *T. rex*, theropods were the terrors of the Mesozoic Era. They are known from all corners of the Earth and existed for 165 million years.

*Allosaurus*

Can you remember which of these theropods ate fish?

*Megalasaurus*

250 mya (million years ago)

**TRIASSIC**

205 mya

**JURASSIC**

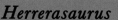

*Herrerasaurus*

Which of the theropods on these pages lived millions of years before the rest?

*Ceratosaurus*

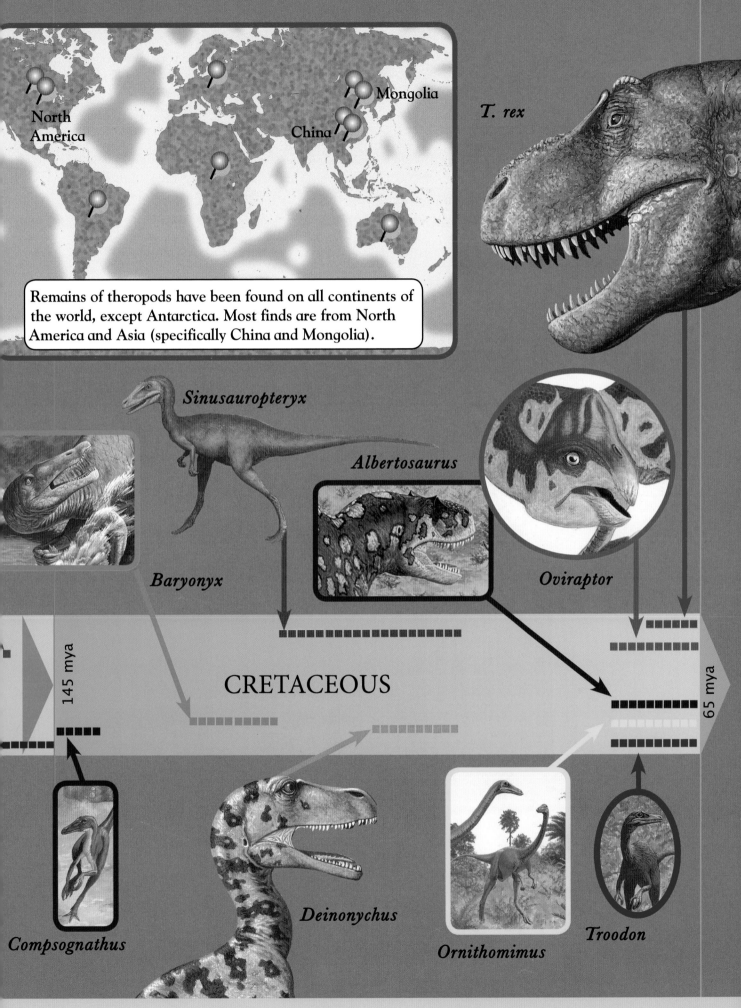

Remains of theropods have been found on all continents of the world, except Antarctica. Most finds are from North America and Asia (specifically China and Mongolia).

North America

Mongolia

China

*T. rex*

*Sinusauropteryx*

*Albertosaurus*

*Oviraptor*

*Baryonyx*

145 mya

CRETACEOUS

65 mya

*Compsognathus*

*Deinonychus*

*Ornithomimus*

*Troodon*

WORLD OF WoW WONDER

## PEGS FOR TEETH 48

## WHERE THEY LIVED 54

## GIANT SKELETONS 56

# LONG-NECKS 58

# DIET 62

# DEFENSE 66

# GIANT PLANT-EATERS

The dinosaur group called the "sauropodomorphs" included the sauropods, which were the huge, long-necked plant-eaters, like *Apatosaurus* and *Diplodocus*, and the earlier, smaller prosauropods, such as *Plateosaurus*.

The most famous of the giant plant-eaters lived in the Late Jurassic period of North America, 150 mya. *Diplodocus* and *Apatosaurus* fed on low plants, while *Brachiosaurus*, with its massively long neck, could reach up into the treetops.

*Brachiosaurus*

*Diplodocus*

## Awesome facts
The bigger kinds of sauropods weighed around 55 tons (49.9 metric tons). But the very biggest ones might have weighed even more.

# PEGS FOR TEETH

Despite their massive size, the sauropods had pretty weak teeth. It's hard to imagine how these enormous plant-eaters managed to break off enough leaves and twigs to survive. Most of them probably never stopped eating.

## BITING BITS

Sauropod teeth were often shaped like pegs or pencils. Some, like *Diplodocus*, only had teeth at the front of the jaws. These were used strictly for biting off plants. Sauropods did not chew food before swallowing.

*Diplodocus*

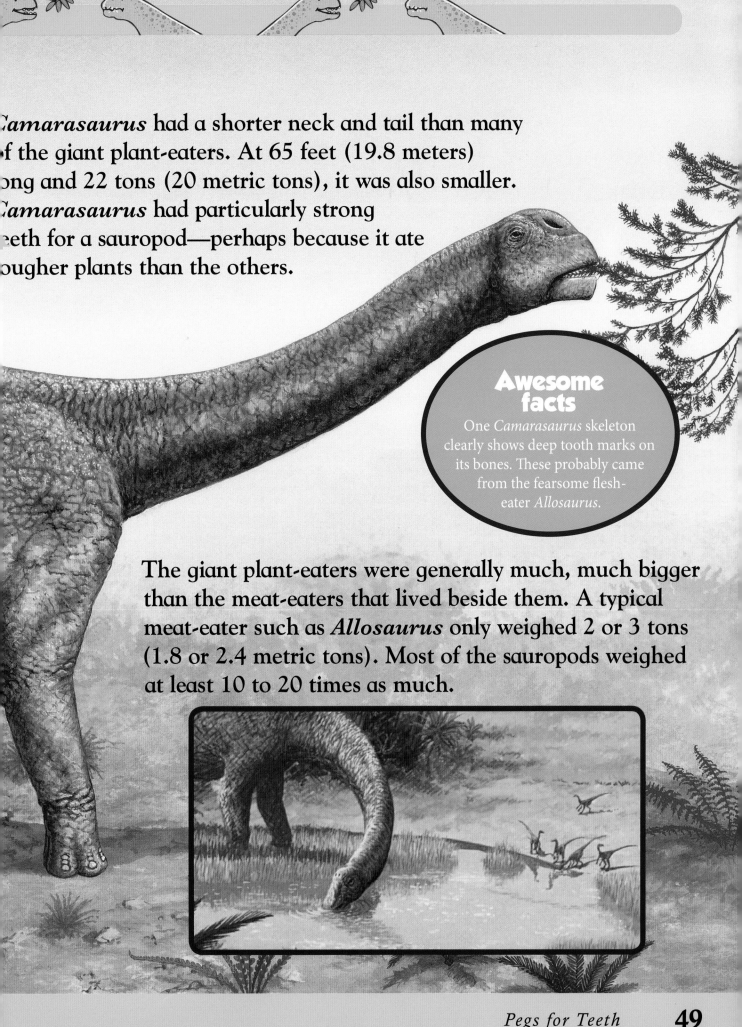

*Camarasaurus* had a shorter neck and tail than many of the giant plant-eaters. At 65 feet (19.8 meters) long and 22 tons (20 metric tons), it was also smaller. *Camarasaurus* had particularly strong teeth for a sauropod—perhaps because it ate tougher plants than the others.

## Awesome facts

One *Camarasaurus* skeleton clearly shows deep tooth marks on its bones. These probably came from the fearsome flesh-eater *Allosaurus*.

The giant plant-eaters were generally much, much bigger than the meat-eaters that lived beside them. A typical meat-eater such as *Allosaurus* only weighed 2 or 3 tons (1.8 or 2.4 metric tons). Most of the sauropods weighed at least 10 to 20 times as much.

# ANCESTORS

The giant sauropods' ancestors were much smaller. An early sauropodomorph was *Thecodontosaurus*, a two-legged, six-foot-long animal from the Late Triassic period of southern England.

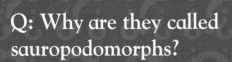

Q: Why are they called sauropodomorphs?

A: "Sauropodomorph" is a bit of a mouthful, meaning "lizard feet forms." The name is not ideal, since their feet are more like elephants' feet than lizards' feet, but it sticks.

The bones of *Thecodontosaurus* were found in 1836 in broken limestone and sandstone from a cave. The animals must have fallen in by accident.

In the cave deposits (above), skeletons of male and female *Thecodontosaurus* adults, as well as the skeleton of a baby, have been found. *Thecodontosaurus* had to look after their young carefully, as there were many big meat-eaters around in the Late Triassic period.

# FEEDING

One of the first giant plant-eaters was the prosauropod *Plateosaurus* from the Late Triassic period of Germany. It used its strong hands and powerful tongue to find the huge amounts of food it needed to survive.

Unusual polished stones have been found inside the rib cages of many dinosaurs. These were probably stomach stones, or gastroliths. Dinosaurs could not chew their food, so they swallowed pebbles, which sat in the stomach and helped to grind up the unchewed food. Modern hens do this by swallowing grit.

*Plateosaurus* had a long, narrow skull. It could open its mouth wide, and used its muscular tongue to grasp leaves. Its small teeth could only cut soft plants.

## HANDS

*Plateosaurus* had five strong fingers. Its thumb was broad and very muscular and had a deep claw on it. It used its hands to rake leaves together before stuffing them into its mouth.

Thumb claw

# WHERE IN THE WORLD?

By the end of the Triassic period, some prosauropods had become huge. *Riojasaurus* from Argentina was 33 feet (10 meters) long. It most likely walked on all fours most of the time, but maybe went up on its hind legs to feed in trees.

In the Late Triassic and Early Jurassic periods, the Atlantic Ocean had not yet begun to open up. This meant that *Riojasaurus* and *Melanorosaurus* could easily walk between what is now South America and South Africa. The land connection existed for another 50 million years.

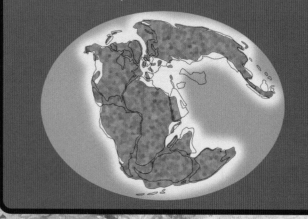

*Riojasaurus* could kill small meat-eaters with one whack of its powerful tail. It could also defend itself by swiping at them with its hands or feet. Its claws were designed for gathering plant food, but they could also deliver a vicious cut.

*Melanorosaurus*, a large prosauropod from the Early Jurassic period of South Africa, was a close relative of *Riojasaurus*. This giant prosauropod is known only from incomplete remains.

*Riojasaurus* had a huge size advantage over meat-eating dinosaurs. However, small meat-eaters may have hunted in packs, perhaps separating young animals from the herd and attacking them.

# SKELETONS

By the Middle Jurassic period, 175 mya, the prosauropods had gone and the sauropods ruled the Earth. One of the first to be found was *Cetiosaurus*, a medium-sized sauropod from England, which measured about 30 feet (9.1 meters) long.

As more skeletons are found, scientists can construct more and more accurate computer models of dinosaurs. These can be animated to show how different dinosaurs moved.

## *CETIOSAURUS* SKELETON

Studies of the neck of *Cetiosaurus* show that it could not bend far upward. So *Cetiosaurus* could only reach up into low trees, perhaps no higher than 6-9 feet (1.8-2.7 meters) above the ground.

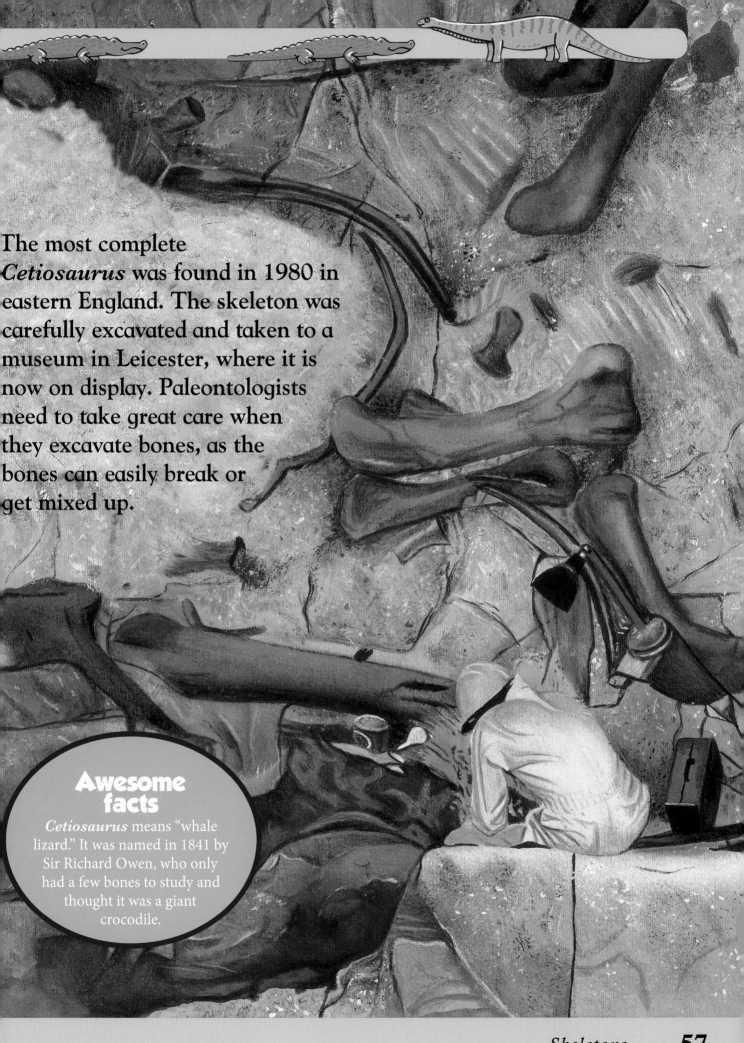

The most complete *Cetiosaurus* was found in 1980 in eastern England. The skeleton was carefully excavated and taken to a museum in Leicester, where it is now on display. Paleontologists need to take great care when they excavate bones, as the bones can easily break or get mixed up.

## Awesome facts

*Cetiosaurus* means "whale lizard." It was named in 1841 by Sir Richard Owen, who only had a few bones to study and thought it was a giant crocodile.

# LONG NECK

Sauropods all had long necks, but *Mamenchisaurus* from the Late Jurassic period of China takes the prize. Its neck was 33 feet (10 meters) long, nearly half its total body length. This might be the longest neck that ever existed on Earth!

## MEDICINE

Dinosaur bones were used as a kind of medicine in China. Villagers ground up these "dragon bones" to make pills that were believed to have therapeutic properties.

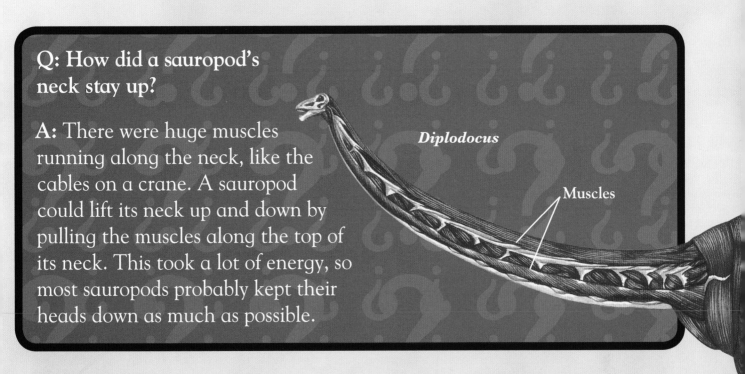

**Q: How did a sauropod's neck stay up?**

**A:** There were huge muscles running along the neck, like the cables on a crane. A sauropod could lift its neck up and down by pulling the muscles along the top of its neck. This took a lot of energy, so most sauropods probably kept their heads down as much as possible.

*Diplodocus*

Muscles

Sauropods used their long necks to reach for food. This means that they did not have to move their massive body when they spotted a tasty bunch of leaves—they just reached out with their neck.

# HUGE AND HEAVY

The heaviest sauropod may have been *Brachiosaurus*, known from the Late Jurassic period of North America and Tanzania in Africa. This monster was 75 feet (22.9 meters) long and weighed as much as 70 tons (63.5 metric tons).

**Q: How did Brachiosaurus support its weight?**

**A:** The skeleton of a sauropod was like a huge bridge. The legs held up the weight and the backbone had high spines over the shoulder and hips. Strong muscles spanned the backbone to balance the long neck and tail.

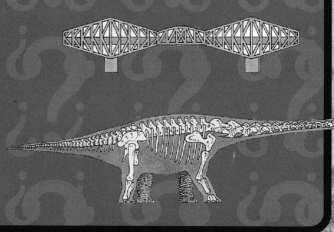

As animals get bigger, their legs get fatter. This is because the legs have to support the increasing weight. Camels have thin legs, elephants have legs like pillars, and sauropods had legs resembling huge tree trunks.

## Awesome facts

Scientists have calculated that, in order to support their vast weight, some sauropods' legs would have been so thick that they would hardly have been able to move.

Scientists debate how high into the trees *Brachiosaurus* could reach. Some say it held its head straight up in the air. However, close study of the neck bones has shown that it probably held its neck at a gentle slope, reaching up to 30 feet (9.1 meters) above the ground.

Sauropods may have had to eat nonstop to stay alive.

# DIET

*Diplodocus* was 88 feet (26.8 meters) long, the longes of the well-known sauropods. This gentle giant must have spent its whole day—and most of the night—munching just to get enough food to survive.

# AMOUNTS OF FOOD

Jurassic plant food was pretty tough—mostly ferns and fern-like plants. A sauropod had to eat vast amounts to get any nourishment. *Diplodocus* might have had to get through 5 tons (4.5 metric tons) of ferns a day—that's a pile as big as a bus!

Some dinosaur bones had growth rings. Each year, another ring was added, just like the rings on a tree. This suggests that the giant sauropods— and possibly the other dinosaurs—were cold-blooded and could grow only in warm weather.

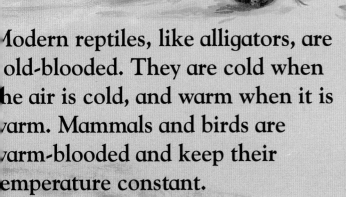

Modern reptiles, like alligators, are cold-blooded. They are cold when the air is cold, and warm when it is warm. Mammals and birds are warm-blooded and keep their temperature constant.

# PLODDING ALONG

A great deal is known about how *Apatosaurus*, from the Late Jurassic period of North America, lived. Skeletons and footprints show that it was not a fast mover. It was a close relative of *Diplodocus*, but not as long—only 70 feet (21.3 meters) from snout to tail tip.

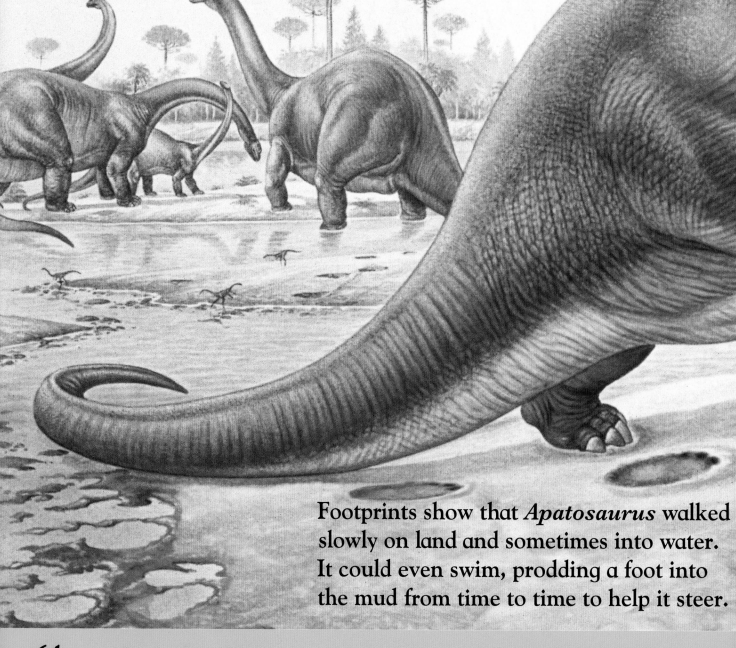

Footprints show that *Apatosaurus* walked slowly on land and sometimes into water. It could even swim, prodding a foot into the mud from time to time to help it steer.

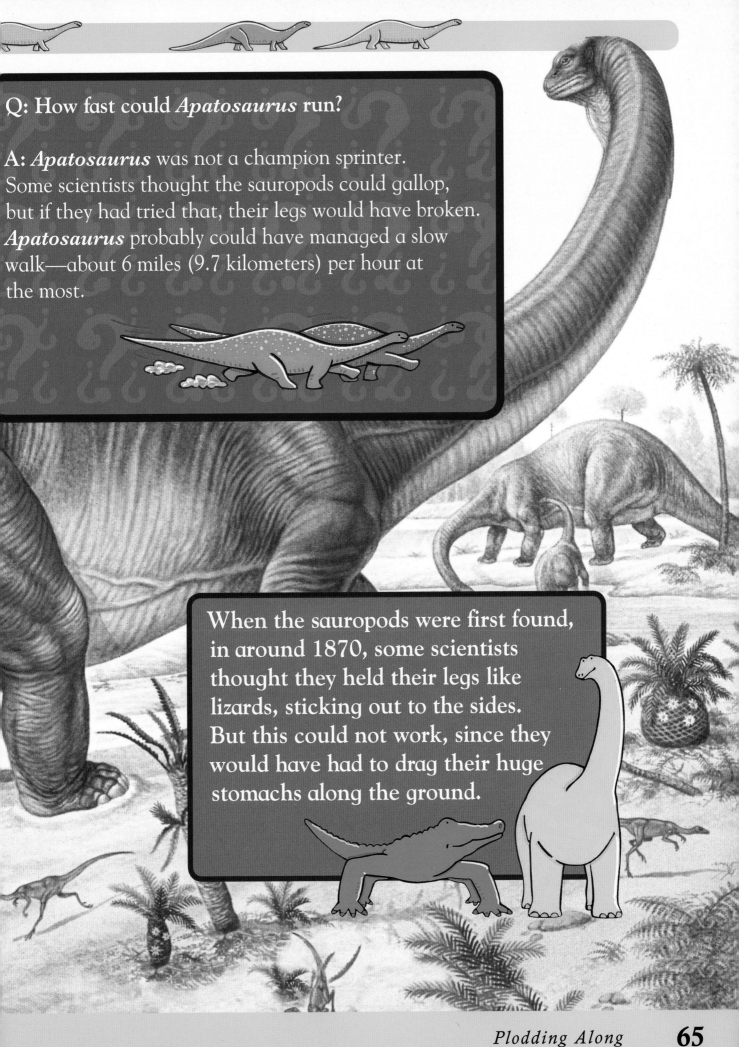

Q: How fast could *Apatosaurus* run?

A: *Apatosaurus* was not a champion sprinter. Some scientists thought the sauropods could gallop, but if they had tried that, their legs would have broken. *Apatosaurus* probably could have managed a slow walk—about 6 miles (9.7 kilometers) per hour at the most.

When the sauropods were first found, in around 1870, some scientists thought they held their legs like lizards, sticking out to the sides. But this could not work, since they would have had to drag their huge stomachs along the ground.

*Plodding Along*   **65**

# DEFENSE

Sauropods were so huge that they should have been safe from the meat-eaters. But by Late Cretaceous times, a group of South American sauropods called "titanosaurs" were under attack from giant meat-eaters. They even developed armor over their bodies for protection.

## SALTASAURUS SCALES

The titanosaur *Saltasaurus* had large, knob-like bone plates along its back, surrounded by a chain mail of smaller, circular, bony plates. It took a lot of biting to get through this armor.

**Q: Why did sauropods have so few predators?**

**A:** Size has its advantages—most meat-eaters think twice about attacking an animal much bigger than they are. They have to balance the benefit of a huge lunch against the risk of being crushed to death. It is much easier to attack smaller beasts!

Sometimes, sauropods might have reared up if they were under attack. They could then have used their vast weight to crush an attacker, or they could have swiped at them with the long claws on their hands.

# GIANT PLANT EATERS' WORLD

The giant plant-eaters dominated the Late Triassic and Jurassic worlds—prosauropods first, then sauropods throughout the Jurassic. In southern continents, the sauropods continued in force right into the Cretaceous period.

*Thecodontosaurus*

*Riojasaurus*

250 mya
(million years ago)

TRIASSIC

205 mya

JURASSIC

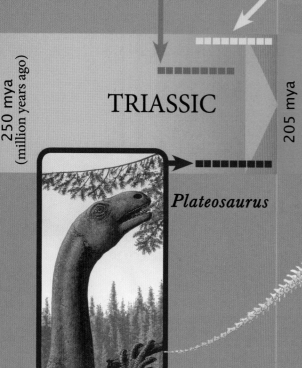

*Plateosaurus*

*Cetiosaurus*

*Apatosaurus*

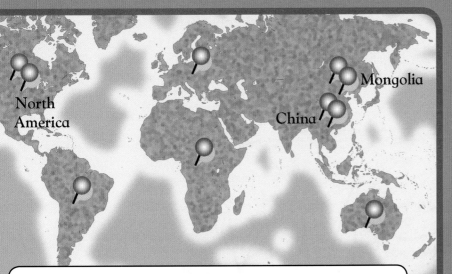

Remains of theropods have been found on all continents of the world, except Antarctica. Most finds are from North America and Asia (specifically China and Mongolia).

North America

Mongolia

China

*Saltasaurus*

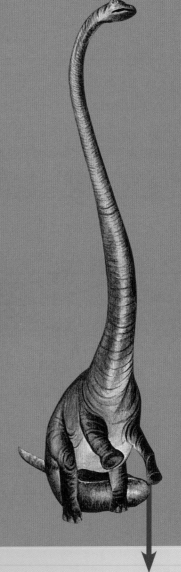

**Which of these sauropods lived right up until the extinction of the dinosaurs, 65 mya?**

*Camarasaurus*

145 mya

CRETACEOUS

65 mya

*Diplodocus*

*Brachiosaurus*

**Can you remember which of these sauropods had the longest neck?**

## DUCKBILLS 74

## IGUANODON 80

## RUNNERS 82

# CRESTS AND SNORKELS 84

# SMACKERS 88

# FAMILY PROTECTION 92

# HORNS, BONES, AND BILLS

Duckbills and their relatives were part of the group of two-legged, plant-eating dinosaurs called "ornithopods." The bonehead group, called "marginocephalians," included the boneheads themselves, called "pachycephalosaurs," and the horn faces, called "ceratopsians."

Duckbills and boneheads were key dinosaurs of
the Cretaceous period. In the Late Cretaceous
period of Canada, herds of the ornithopod
*Lambeosaurus* lived alongside
the ceratopsian *Styracosaurus* and the
smaller pachycephalosaur *Stegoceras*.
All the duckbills and boneheads were
plant-eaters.

Lambeosaurus

Styracosaurus

When is a duck not a duck? When it's a duckbill.

# WHAT MAKES A DUCKBILL?

Duckbilled dinosaurs called "hadrosaurs" were the most successful dinosaurs of all. Hundreds of their skeletons have been found in Late Cretaceous rocks in China, North America, and Mongolia. Hadrosaurs had much the same body, but the heads were very different, often with bizarre crests.

Although hadrosaurs looked like ducks, and may have been able to swim, they spent most of their time running about on dry land. Their huge tails were used for balance. Thin rods of bone called "ossified tendons" ran along the tail and over the hips. These helped to keep the tail stiff.

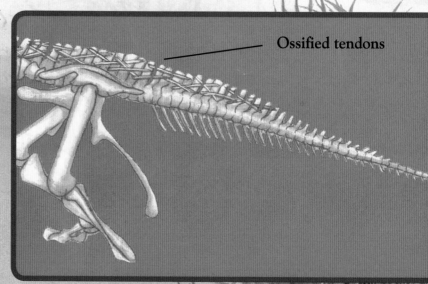

Ossified tendons

# DUCKBILL TEETH

Duckbills had hundreds of teeth arranged in tight rows, all designed for chopping tough plants. Some had as many as 2,000 teeth in total.

*Corythosaurus*

One of the best-known duckbills, *Corythosaurus* of North America, had a crest shaped like half a plate on its head. It had small hooves on its fingers and toes, suggesting that it walked on all fours. However, *Corythosaurus* also used its hands for grabbing food.

# EARLY ORNITHOPODS

The duckbills were common in the Late Cretaceous period, but the ornithopod group had been around since the Triassic period. The early ones were small and fast-moving, so they could escape from predators.

*Lesothosaurus*

*Lesothosaurus* had five fingers on its hand, just like a human, which shows that it was a primitive form. Most dinosaurs born later had only three or four fingers. *Lesothosaurus* used its strong little hands to gather leaves, and maybe even to carry them off, if it was disturbed.

Q: What did Lesothosaurus eat?

A: Like all ornithopods, it ate plants. As it closed its jaws, its teeth rubbed firmly against each other. Its teeth could cut plant stems like a large pair of scissors.

*Heterodontosaurus*

*Heterodontosaurus* means "different-tooth lizard." It had long canine teeth, similar to a dog. These were not used for piercing flesh, but probably for grasping tough plant stems.

Canine teeth

# LONG-DISTANCE JOURNEYS

By the Middle of the Jurassic period, duckbills and their relatives lived worldwide. One famous one, *Dryosaurus,* was found in North America in 1894. A similar dinosaur was discovered in Tanzania, Africa, in 1919. By 1970, it was realized that they were identical.

Middle Jurassic

North America

Atlantic Ocean opens up

Possible migration routes

Africa

Identical dinosaurs across the world means long-distance migration. The Atlantic Ocean only began to open in the Middle Jurassic. Before then, *Dryosaurus* could easily have hiked from America to Africa on dry land.

Plant-eaters often migrated huge distances in search of food. In hot, dry climates, they might have followed the wet seasons north and south to maintain a constant supply of leaves.

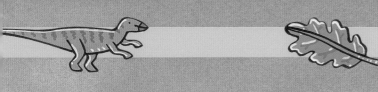

# DINOSAUR DUNG

How do we know what dinosaurs like *Dryosaurus* ate? Fossils of dung, called "coprolite," have been found with chopped up leaves and stalks in them. Like horses, dinosaurs probably couldn't digest it all, so some came out in their dung.

*Dryosaurus* had strong arms that it used to reach leaves. Its jaws were lined with broad teeth, good for chopping up stems. But it had special feature, seen in all the dinosaurs of the ornithopod group—a horny beak at the front of the jaws, which it used to cut and bite plants.

*Dryosaurus*

# NAMING THE BEAST

Many skeletons of the ornithopod *Iguanodon* have been found in Early Cretaceous rocks in southern England, Belgium, France, and Germany. *Iguanodon* had a wicked thumb spike, which it may have used to defend itself.

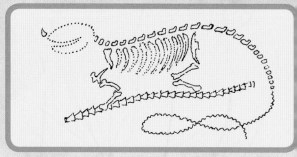

Early collectors only had a few bones of *Iguanodon*, and they thought a heavy, pointed bone was a nose horn (above). Only when whole skeletons were found in 1877 did they see that this bone was in fact the thumb spike.

## Awesome facts

From examination of fossil feet, paleontologists think that *Iguanodon* may have suffered from arthritis in its ankles.

*Iguanodon* was named by Gideon Mantell in 1825. His wife, Mary Ann, had found some teeth in a pile of rubble beside a road in southern England. He later found more bones in a quarry nearby. The name means "iguana tooth," since Mantell thought its teeth were like those of the modern iguana lizard.

*Iguanodon*

# RUNNERS

*Hypsilophodon* was a small, fast-moving ornithopod. Great herds of them lived in southern England, and close relatives have been found all over the world. They were among the most successful dinosaurs of their day.

*Hypsilophodon*

Stride length

Length of leg

Dinosaur speeds can be calculated by looking at their leg skeletons and footprints. When an animal runs faster, it takes longer strides—just like you! If you know the stride length (measured from fossil tracks) and the length of the leg, then you can work out the speed.

**Awesome facts**

*Hypsilophodon* could run at a speed of 20 miles (32.2 kilometers) per hour or more, which is about the same speed as a racehorse, have suffered from arthritis in its ankles.

**Q: Did *Hypsilophodon* hide in trees?**

**A:** Some old reconstructions show *Hypsilophodon* perching in a tree. This would have been impossible, however, because its feet would not have been able to grasp a branch. *Hypsilophodon* certainly hid from predators in bushes and found food among the trees, but it was definitely not an oversized perching bird!

# CRESTS AND SNORKELS

The duckbills of the Late Cretaceous period, the hadrosaurs, are famous for their amazing headgear— a huge range of crests, horns, and snorkel-like tubes. Scientists have debated what they were for. They may have marked different species by their various shapes and sounds.

*Parasaurolophus*

*Corythosaurus*

Different crests made different noises. Each hadrosaur had its own special honk or squeak. In a herd of many different species, hadrosaurs of different types could look and listen for their mates.

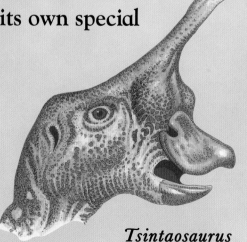

*Tsintaosaurus*

Males and females of a species also had different crest shapes, so they looked and sounded a bit different from each other. One of the *Parasaurolophus* had a shorter crest than the other, but scientists don't know whether the short-crested form was the male or the female.

*Parasaurolophus* had one of the most amazing crests—a long tube on top of its head. This was once thought to be a snorkel that allowed the dinosaur to breathe underwater, but there was no hole at the end. It probably allowed one *Parasaurolophus* to identify another.

*Parasaurolophus*

## INSIDE THE CREST

The breathing tubes in a crest ran up from the nostrils to the end of the crest, then back and down to the throat. When a hadrosaur breathed in or out, the air went all around this long set of tubes. This would have made a noise, since the tubes were like part of a trumpet.

Air

# PARENTS

Amazing discoveries have been made recently about how duckbills looked after their young. *Maiasaura* of North America cared for their little hatchlings and fed them softened plant fragments. *"Maiasaura"* means "good mother lizard."

## Awesome facts

*Maiasaura* hatchlings were 3 feet (0.9 meters) long before they left the nest. Until then, their moms brought them tender shoots and leaves to eat.

## INSIDE A DINOSAUR EGG

Before hatching, a dinosaur baby was very tightly coiled inside the egg. Paleontologists have found some dinosaur eggs that even contain the tiny bones of an embryo that had died inside.

Embryo

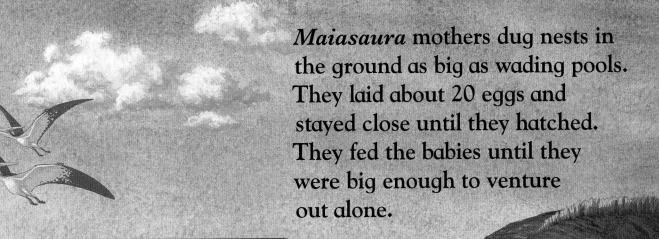

*Maiasaura* mothers dug nests in the ground as big as wading pools. They laid about 20 eggs and stayed close until they hatched. They fed the babies until they were big enough to venture out alone.

**Q: Some birds nest in trees, so why didn't dinosaurs?**

**A:** The dinosaur mom would first have had to find a strong tree, then she would have had to climb up somehow. Most dinosaurs were simply too big, or not nimble enough to manage this.

# SMACKERS

The boneheads called "pachycephalosaurs," meaning "thick-head lizards," are famous for having very thick skull roofs. The males may have had head-butting fights.

## DOMEHEADS

There were two groups of pachycephalosaurs—one set with very thick, domed skull roofs, and the other with lower, flatter skull roofs.

Stegoceras

Just like boneheads, modern mountain goats crash heads to see who is strongest, in fights for territory or mates.

Pachycephalosaurs arose in the Early Cretaceous period, but they are best known from the Late Cretaceous period of North America and central Asia. They ran around on two legs, and were plant-eaters.

The horn faces, called "ceratopsians," probably head-butted each other. They may have sized each other up, trying to scare their rival away by appearing fierce. They roared and may even have changed the color of the bony frill around their neck. If that didn't work, they may have then crashed heads and tussled.

Styracosaurus

# YOUNG AND OLD

Skeletons of baby dinosaurs show they were like human babies— big heads, big eyes, short legs, and knobby knees. One of the best series of family fossils found is of the ceratopsian *Protoceratops*, from the Late Cretaceous period.

An amazing set of fossil tracks from North America shows how a herd protected its young. The tiny footprints of the babies are in the middle, with the bigger moms' and dads' footprints on the outside.

Fossil specimens from Mongolia include dozens of skulls of whole families of *Protoceratops*. Of course, the dinosaur became bigger as it grew older, but the shape of the skull also changed. The babies had huge eyes, short beaks, and weak jaws.

Baby

Juvenile

Adult

An amazing fossil specimen, found in Mongolia in the 1960s, shows a *Protoceratops* and a *Velociraptor* locked in mortal combat. They were killed by a sandstorm.

Protoceratops

One ceratopsian, *Torosaurus*, had a head as long as a car.

# FAMILY PROTECTION

Sometimes there is safety in numbers. Similar to musk oxen today, ceratopsians may have formed a ring with their horned heads outward when a meat-eater threatened. Many plant-eaters could use the herd as a way to protect themselves.

*Einiosaurus*

*Albertosaurus*

*Styracosaurus*

Even on their own, the ceratopsians were able to look after themselves. *Albertosaurus* had to be careful when it was faced by the long nose horn and spiky frill of *Styracosaurus*.

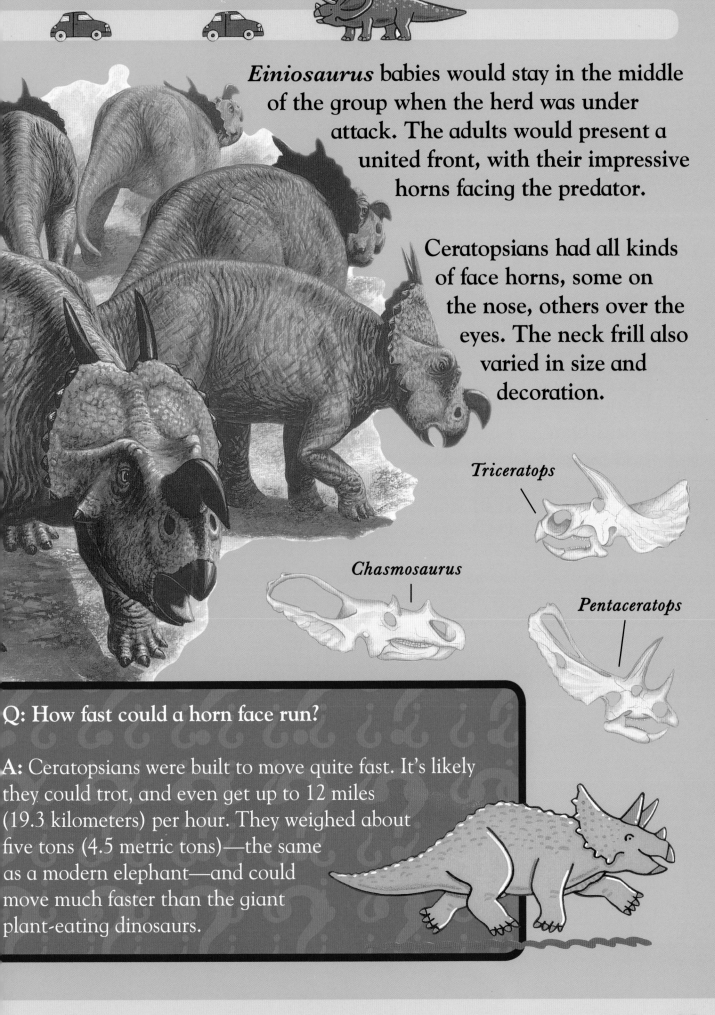

*Einiosaurus* babies would stay in the middle of the group when the herd was under attack. The adults would present a united front, with their impressive horns facing the predator.

Ceratopsians had all kinds of face horns, some on the nose, others over the eyes. The neck frill also varied in size and decoration.

*Triceratops*

*Chasmosaurus*

*Pentaceratops*

**Q: How fast could a horn face run?**

**A:** Ceratopsians were built to move quite fast. It's likely they could trot, and even get up to 12 miles (19.3 kilometers) per hour. They weighed about five tons (4.5 metric tons)—the same as a modern elephant—and could move much faster than the giant plant-eating dinosaurs.

# DUCKBILL AND BONEHEAD WORLD

Ornithopods peaked in the Cretaceous period, from *Iguanodon* to the later duckbills. The boneheads (pachycephalosaurs) and horned ceratopsians are only really known from the Late Cretaceous period.

Which ornithopod had long canine teeth like a dog?

Can you remember which duckbill had long canine teeth like a dog?

*Dryosaurus*

Which two ornithopods on these pages lived millions of years before the rest?

250 mya
(Million years ago)

TRIASSIC

205 mya

JURASSIC

*Lesothosaurus*

*Heterodontosaur*

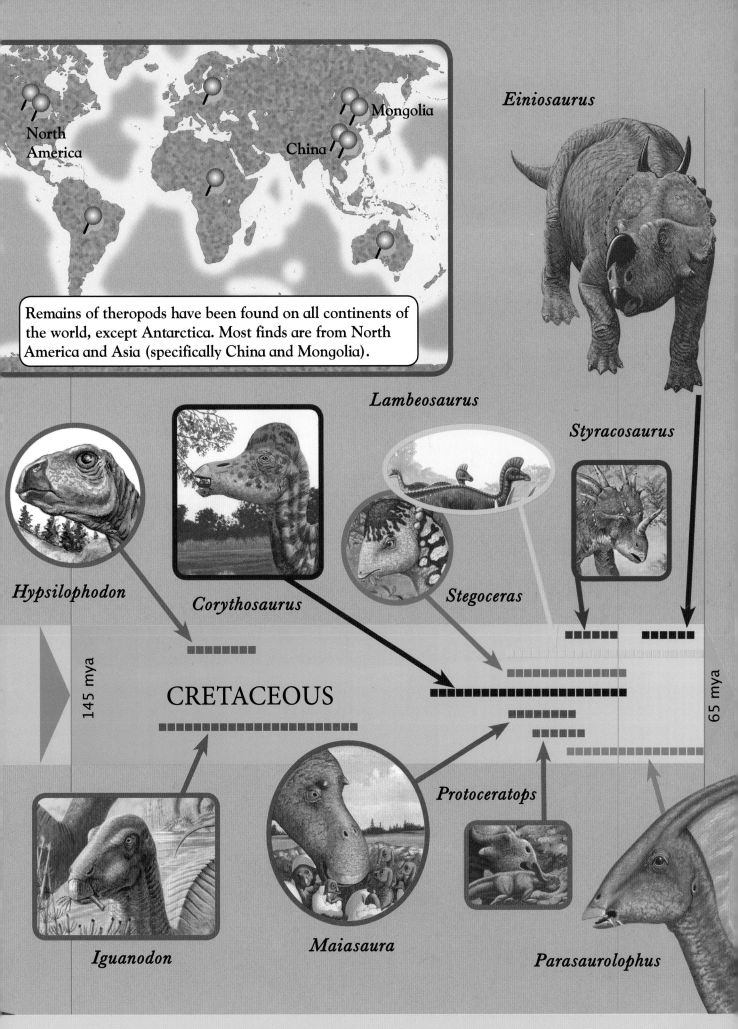

Einiosaurus

Remains of theropods have been found on all continents of the world, except Antarctica. Most finds are from North America and Asia (specifically China and Mongolia).

Mongolia

China

North America

Lambeosaurus

Styracosaurus

Hypsilophodon

Corythosaurus

Stegoceras

145 mya

CRETACEOUS

65 mya

Protoceratops

Iguanodon

Maiasaura

Parasaurolophus

## BACK PLATES 100

## MONSTER MUSEUM 104

## WALKING WORKS 110

# SUPER DINO 114

# BONED UP 116

# FIGHTING
# 118

# ARMORED DINOSAURS

The armored dinosaurs, called "thyreophorans," lived through the Jurassic and Cretaceous periods. The stegosaurs were particularly important during the Late Jurassic period and the ankylosaurs flourished during the Cretaceous period.

Ankylosaurs, such as *Hylaeosaurus*, were covered in bony armor and some had large spines along their sides. Stegosaurs, such as *Kentrosaurus*, had spines and plates down the middle of their backs.

*Hylaeosaurus*

The stegosaurs all had different arrangements of armor plates. *Stegosaurus* from the Late Jurassic period of North America had broad plates on its back and tail spikes. *Kentrosaurus* from Tanzania and *Tuojiangosaurus* from China had spines.

*Stegosaurus*

*Tuojiangosaurus*

# PLATES ON END

The most famous stegosaur, *Stegosaurus*, had broad, flat plates down its back. People once thought the plates lay flat to form a kind of shell, but markings at the base of the plates show that they stood upright. What were they for?

## SMALL BRAINS

*Stegosaurus* is known as the least intelligent dinosaur. It had a brain the size of a walnut. There was actually a second "brain" in the hip region, which operated the hind legs and tail.

Second "brain"

A *Stegosaurus* could trot along at about 9 miles (14.5 kilometers) per hour. They weren't built for speed, but relied on their plates and spikes for protection.

The plates on *Stegosaurus* were for protection and temperature control. Fossils show they were covered with skin and had large blood vessels. When *Stegosaurus* was angry or hot, it pumped blood over the plates. This made them flush red and also shed heat.

Blood vessels

# EARLY TROTTERS

The first armored dinosaur was from the Early Jurassic period of southern England. Called *"Scelidosaurus,"* paleontologists have debated for years whether it is a stegosaur or an ankylosaur—it seems to have been ancestor to both groups.

Scelidosaurus was a sleek animal, about 13 feet (four meters) long. It trotted around on all fours, seeking ferns and other low plants. Scientists think that it evolved from a two-legged ancestor, since the hind legs are much longer than the front legs. There were seven main rows of bony spines running the length of the body.

## COMPLETE SKELETON

*Scelidosaurus* was the first complete dinosaur skeleton and one of the first armored forms ever discovered. It was named in 1860 by Sir Richard Owen.

recent specimen of *Scelidosaurus*, on display at the Bristol City Museum in England, shows excellent detail of the skull. Some of the skin has even been preserved. The pattern on the skin shows a kind of chain mail of many bony plates all over it.

*Scelidosaurus* nipped off leaves, then pulled them back into its mouth with its tongue. The cheek pouches saved it from losing bits of food out of the sides.

# MONSTER MUSEUM

Many dinosaurs have been found in China since 1970. One of the most spectacular sites is the *Dashanpu* Quarry at Zigong in Sichuan province, where a group of dinosaurs from the Middle Jurassic period has been unearthed. A key discovery was the stegosaur *Tuojiangosaurus*, of which 12 skeletons exist.

*Armored Dinosaurs*

he Zigong site was discovered
y Dong Zhiming, a leading
Chinese
paleontologist
based in
Beijing. He has
named many
amazing new
dinosaurs.

he Zigong Dinosaur Museum
isplays skeletons mounted in the
sual way, but visitors can also look
t some skeletons that are still in
he rock. This gives people an idea
f what paleontologists see when
hey first discover fossilized bones.

# LEAF-EATERS

Stegosaurs were plant-eaters. They fed on low bushes and trees, tearing out leaves and chomping them. However, they mostly ate soft leaves, since their teeth were not very powerful.

Stegosaurs probably ate ferns as well as seed ferns close to the ground, and the lower leaves of conifer trees, such as the monkey puzzle tree. There were no deciduous trees or flowering plants in the Late Jurassic period.

*Kentrosaurus*, from the Late Jurassic period of Tanzania in Africa, may have been able to rear up and snatch leaves from low levels in trees The sauropods *Barosaurus* and *Brachiosaurus* fed at higher levels.

## STEGOSAUR TEETH

Stegosaurs had long, narrow jaws and teeth that were quite short. The jaws were not built for chomping twigs and tough plant food, nor were the teeth—the teeth had a scalloped edge that was very useful for cutting leaves.

*Gasosaurus* was found in an area of China called "Sichuan."

Gasosaurus

# SQUARING UP

It seems certain that armored dinosaurs used their armor to stand up to predators. *Huayangosaurus,* a stegosaur from the Middle Jurassic period of China, could face up to the meat-eater *Gasosaurus* just by looking scary.

Stegosaurs might have used their sharp spines to square up to rivals as well. The bigger dino probably scared the smaller one away.

*Huayangosaurus*

**Q: What could a stegosaur do with its tail?**

**A:** Whack its enemies! A stegosaur had powerful muscles in its tail, and it could deliver a wounding blow. A meat-eater could get a slash up to 3 feet long (0.9 meters) in its flesh. No thanks!

Stegosaurs were mostly placid animals, but an attacker would face a furious defense—red-flushing spines and plates, and a wickedly spiked, swiping tail.

# WALKING WORKS

The ankylosaurs were slow movers and were smaller than the stegosaurs. They didn't have to move fast— with a heavy armor of plates all over their body, they were safe from attackers. Even if it wanted to, an ankylosaur couldn't shift all that weight at any faster than a stroll.

Fossilized tracks show that ankylosaurs moved slowly. The footprints are close together, suggesting that the maximum speed they could reach was perhaps 6 miles (9.7 kilometers) per hour— the same speed you go when you jog. You could beat one in a sprint race!

*Polacanthus*

110 *Armored Dinosaurs*

## THICK LEGS

Ankylosaurs had short, fat legs with unusually broad and short bones. The bones had to be stout to support the great weight of all the armor.

*Polacanthus* and *Hylaeosaurus* lived in mixed herds in the Early Cretaceous period of southern England. These two dinosaurs were very similar, except they had different patterns on their armor.

# FLOWER CHOMPERS

The ankylosaurs lived mainly in lowland areas near lakes and rivers. They fed on lush plants around these watery habitats, but could not reach up high into trees or go up on their hind legs.

Q: Why did some ankylosaurs have broader mouths than others?

A: The shape of their mouths tells us about the food they ate. A broad mouth, like *Sauropelta's*, means it cropped all kinds of plants and flowers. A narrow mouth, like *Polacanthus'*, means it probably only ate certain low-lying plants.

*Polacanthus*

During the Cretaceous period, there were big changes in plant life. The earliest ankylosaurs fed on ferns, seed ferns, and low conifers, but the group really took off after the flowering plants appeared in the Mid-Cretaceous period. The ankylosaurs would have especially liked the new plants—early roses, vines, and magnolias.

*Sauropelta*

*Sauropelta*, from the Mid-Cretaceous period of North America, lived side-by-side with the meat-eater *Deinonychus*. But the ankylosaur ignored the slashing attacks of the predator— if *Deinonychus* tried any nonsense, it would just break its claws on *Sauropelta*'s armored back.

# SUPER DINO

One of the scariest ankylosaurs was *Edmontonia*. Powerful and sturdy, this ankylosaur also sprouted great spines along its sides. It was about 20 feet (6.1 meters) long, and weighed up to 11 tons (10 metric tons). Attackers would think twice before tackling such a monster!

A baby *Edmontonia* may have seemed a tasty meal for a meat-eater, but the parents would soon scare it off.

*Albertosaurus*

*Edmontonia*

# TANK FEATURES

In the beginning, ankylosaurs resembled turtles, but much, much bigger. *Edmontonia* was one of the biggest ankylosaurs, and was built like an army tank. It couldn't move very fast, but with its great weight, powerful legs and fearsome armor, it must have been unstoppable.

Viewed head-on, *Edmontonia* was an amazing sight, with a tiny armor-plated head and a massive body with forward-pointing spines. Its main enemy, *Albertosaurus*, would know to keep clear.

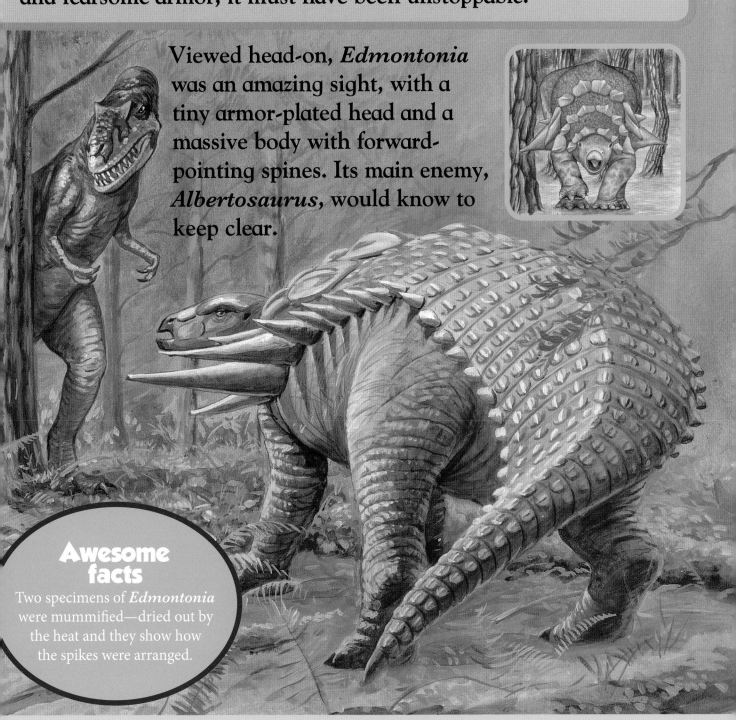

## Awesome facts

Two specimens of *Edmontonia* were mummified—dried out by the heat and they show how the spikes were arranged.

# BONED UP

Ankylosaurs were the best protected animals of all time. Even the head had its own special armor plating. *Talarurus*, of the Late Cretaceous period of Mongolia, is a typical ankylosaur. It was protected from its predators by armor, bony spines, and a bony ball on the end of its tail.

Ankylosaurs had a special pattern of armor plates over their heads. There was a second layer of bones over the normal skull bones. The armor plating even extended to special bony ridges over the nostrils and a bony eyelid cover. No predator could possibly bite through all that!

*Talarurus*

Q: Did *Talarurus* have more bones than other dinosaurs?

A: A typical dinosaur had about 350 bones in its skull and skeleton. Ankylosaurs, like Talarurus, had far more—their armor could add about 300 major bony plates and spines along the back, plus 50 or so extra bone plates around the head, and hundreds of small bone plates in the skin. An adult human has only about 206 bones.

## Awesome facts

Ankylosaurs had so much armor that the skeleton and armor together could make up more than half the dinosaur's total body weight.

# FIGHTING

Ankylosaur armor was for defense, but also for fighting. Male ankylosaurs probably fought their predators and each other. Unlike *Hylaeosaurus* and *Sauropelta,* with their straight tails, *Talarurus* and *Euoplocephalus* had bony tail clubs to fight with.

## INSIDE THE CREST

The breathing tubes in a crest ran up from the nostrils to the end of the crest, then back and down to the throat.

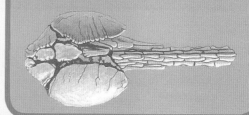

*Euoplocephalus* from the Late Cretaceous of North America lived at the same time as the meat-eater *Carnotaurus*. They must have faced each other often, but after it had been whacked about a bit, *Carnotaurus* would probably have learned not to tackle the ankylosaur.

The tail club was like a steel wrecking ball used to demolish walls. Ankylosaurs could kill predators with their tail clubs if they hit them hard enough in the right place.

Male ankylosaurs probably fought rivals by posing and roaring. The smaller one would eventually be scared off. If the two were equally matched, they might barge into each other, whacking with their tails. But the armor would protect them from serious injury.

# ARMORED DINOSAUR WORLD

The armored dinosaurs split into two groups in the Middle Jurassic period—the plated stegosaurs and the bone-covered ankylosaurs. Stegosaurs were important in the Late Jurassic period, ankylosaurs in the Late Cretaceous period.

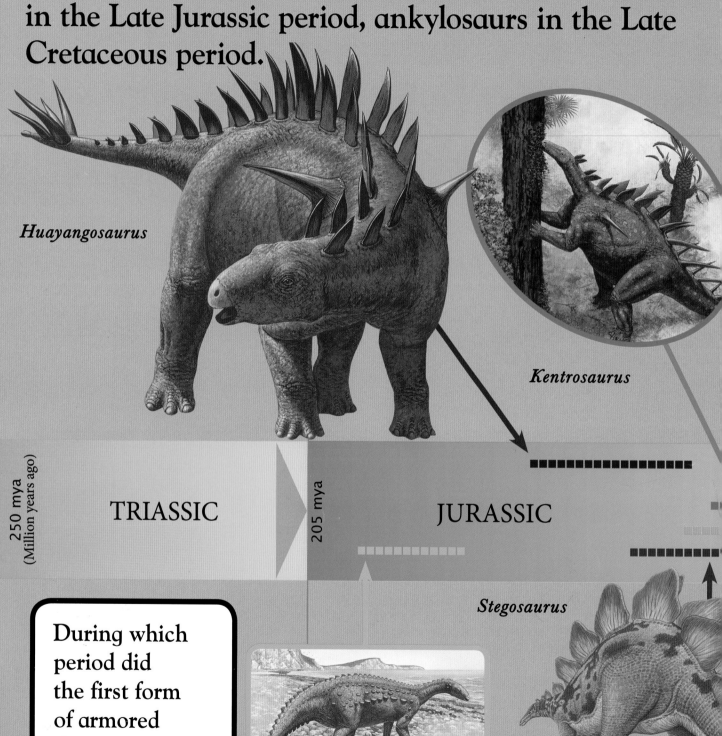

*Huayangosaurus*

*Kentrosaurus*

250 mya (Million years ago)

205 mya

TRIASSIC

JURASSIC

*Stegosaurus*

During which period did the first form of armored dinosaur appear?

*Scelidosaurus*

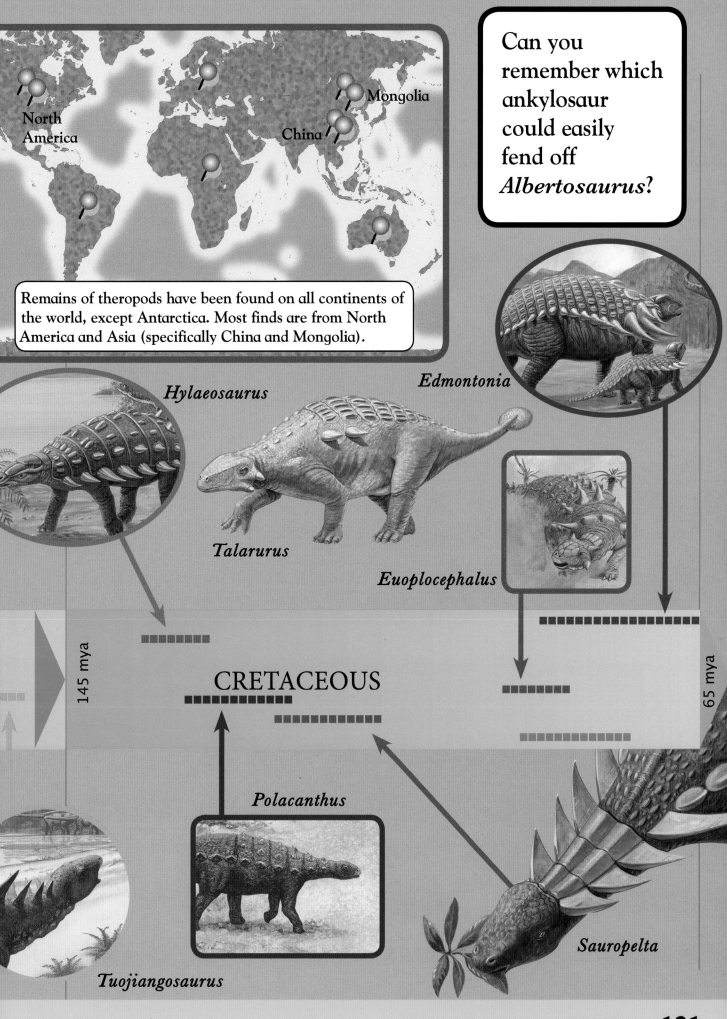

**Can you remember which ankylosaur could easily fend off *Albertosaurus*?**

North America

Mongolia

China

Remains of theropods have been found on all continents of the world, except Antarctica. Most finds are from North America and Asia (specifically China and Mongolia).

*Edmontonia*

*Hylaeosaurus*

*Talarurus*

*Euoplocephalus*

145 mya

CRETACEOUS

65 mya

*Polacanthus*

*Tuojiangosaurus*

*Sauropelta*

PLESIOSAURS 126

ICHTHYOSAURS 128

PTEROSAURS 130

# WHERE DID THEY GO? 134

# RISE OF THE MAMMALS 138

# DINOSAURS TODAY 146

# ALONGSIDE THE DINOSAURS

Dinosaurs were not the only animals alive in the Mesozoic era. Many smaller creatures lived around ponds and in the undergrowth—frogs, turtles, lizards, crocodiles, and mammals. By the Cretaceous period, snakes and birds had also appeared.

During the Mid-Cretaceous period, many of the huge dinosaurs could walk past a whole scene of modern-looking animals, hardly knowing they were there. All kinds of fish swam in ponds, and insects crawled and flew around.

*Liopleurodon* was an amazing four feet (1.2 meters) long.

# PLESIOSAURS

The plesiosaurs were a successful group of marine reptiles that lived throughout the Mesozoic era. There were two kinds—the long-necked plesiosaurs and the short-necked, massive pliosaurs. But these were not dinosaurs.

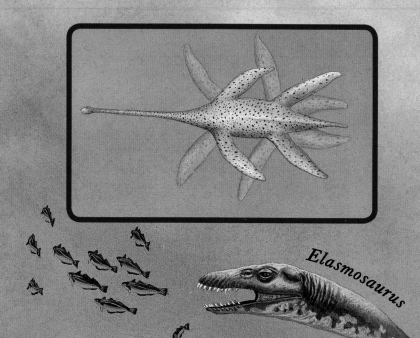

*Elasmosaurus*

Plesiosaurs, such as *Elasmosaurus*, propelled themselves by a kind of underwater flying (above). They moved their strong fins back and down, then turned them and brought them up and forward in a great curved loop.

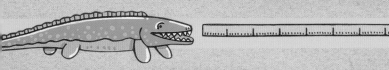

Q: What did plesiosaurs eat?

A: Plesiosaurs ate fish, ammonites, nautiloids, and belemnites. Belemnites, like nautiloids, were ancient, squid-like creatures, with a bullet-like internal skeleton. Ammonites were coiled shellfish, which were also related to modern squids.

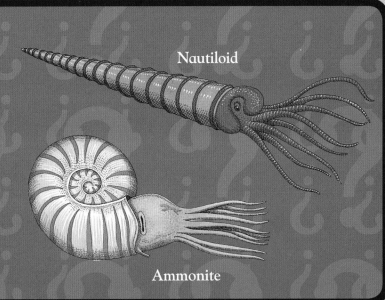

Nautiloid

Ammonite

*Mososaurus*

*Liopleurodon*

The pliosaurs, such as *Liopleurodon*, had massive skulls. They fed on other marine reptiles, such as smaller plesiosaurs and ichthyosaurs. The lizard-like *Mososaurus* was one of the last sea reptiles. It also fed on other marine reptiles, as well as ammonites and fish.

# ICHTHYOSAURS

Ichthyosaurs were amazing marine reptiles. They were completely adapted to life at sea, with streamlined bodies, powerful tail fins, and long snouts. They lived through the Triassic and Jurassic periods, but died out before the end of the Cretaceous period.

Although they look like fish, ichthyosaurs were reptiles and had to breathe air. They probably came to the surface every few minutes for a gulp of air.

Ichthyosaurs could not come out on land to lay eggs, so they gave birth at sea. Some amazing fossils show the mother ichthyosaur in the process of giving birth to live young, just like a dolphin.

## Awesome facts

There are some astonishing fossils of mother ichthyosaurs with as many as 10 unborn babies inside the body.

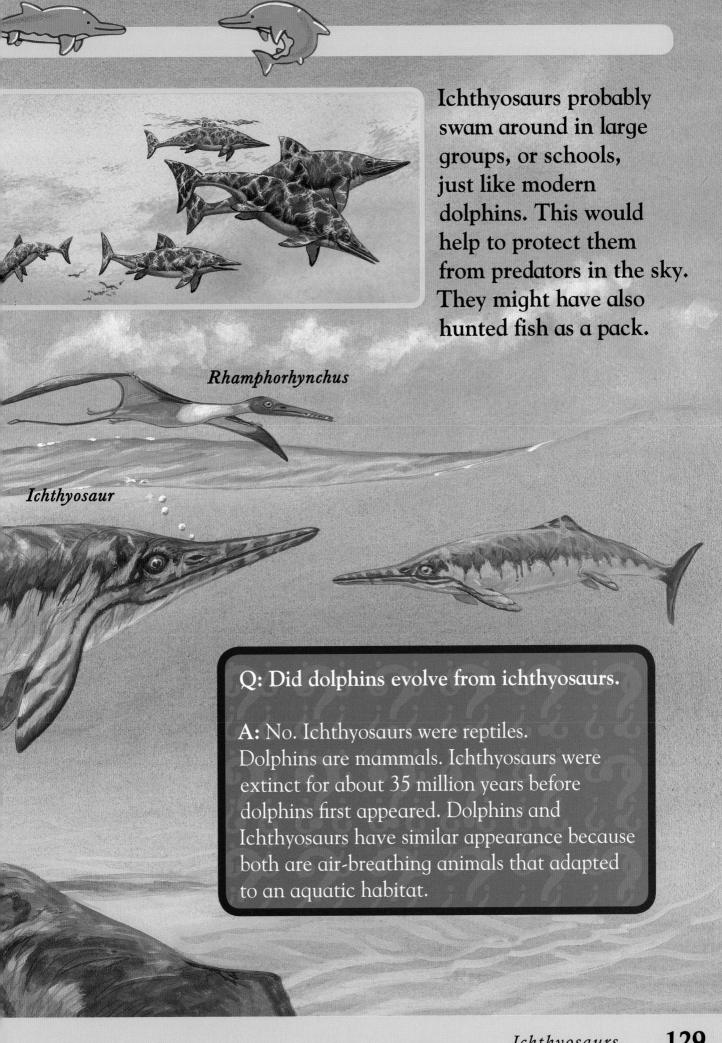

Ichthyosaurs probably swam around in large groups, or schools, just like modern dolphins. This would help to protect them from predators in the sky. They might have also hunted fish as a pack.

*Rhamphorhynchus*

*Ichthyosaur*

Q: Did dolphins evolve from ichthyosaurs.

A: No. Ichthyosaurs were reptiles. Dolphins are mammals. Ichthyosaurs were extinct for about 35 million years before dolphins first appeared. Dolphins and Ichthyosaurs have similar appearance because both are air-breathing animals that adapted to an aquatic habitat.

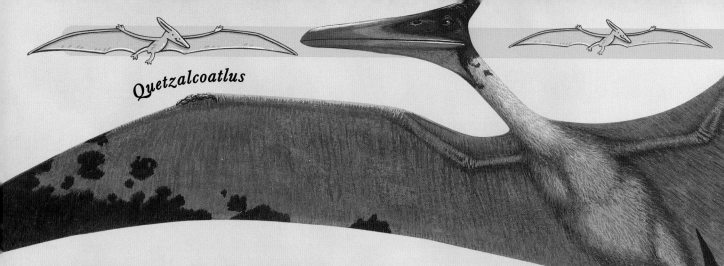

Quetzalcoatlus

# PTEROSAURS

Pterosaurs, or "winged lizards," were a common sight in the Mesozoic era, soaring high over the heads of the dinosaurs. Like marine reptiles, pterosaurs were not dinosaurs, but they were closely related.

Many pterosaurs ate insects, but the larger ones all seem to have been fish-eaters. Some of them skimmed over the waves and scooped fish out. Others dive-bombed into the water, snapping at unsuspecting fish.

Dimorphodon

Rhamphorhynchus

Pteranodon

Baby pterosaurs hatched from eggs that were laid in nests, probably on cliff tops. The parents brought back fish and other morsels for them. It probably took some time before the babies were big and strong enough to fly by themselves.

Q: Did modern birds evolve from pterosaurs.

A: No. Though pterosaurs and birds look similar, they have different skeletal structures and are not related.

# WINGSPAN

Pterosaurs ranged in size from tiny ones to real giants. *Quetzalcoatlus* had a wingspan of 40 feet (12.2 meters) or more—much bigger than any modern bird.

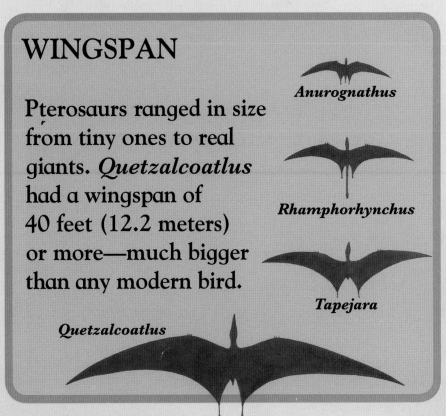

*Anurognathus*

*Rhamphorhynchus*

*Tapejara*

*Quetzalcoatlus*

# BIRDS

Cretaceous skies were full of birds as well as pterosaurs. *Archaeopteryx*, the first bird, lived in the Late Jurassic period of Germany. More and more bird groups appeared during the Cretaceous period, but most of the modern bird groups came later.

Modern birds have short, bony parts to their tail, no teeth, and no hand claws. *Archaeopteryx* is the perfect "missing link" between modern birds and the dinosaurs. It had feathers and wings, but it also had a long, bony tail, teeth in its jaws, and hands on its wings.

*Archaeopteryx*

Several fossilized feathers have been found, which show every detail of the structure of the feather, but not its color. There are now seven fossils of *Archaeopteryx*, all showing the feathers in place. This is how we know it had wings just like a modern bird.

# WHERE DID THEY GO?

The world of the dinosaurs came to an end quite suddenly 65 mya. Scientists are still debating what happened. How could such an amazing group of beasts as the dinosaurs suddenly become extinct?

**Q: Did mammals eat all the dinosaurs' eggs?**

**A:** One theory for the extinction was that mammals ate all the dinosaurs' eggs. But the mammals had been around all through the age of the dinosaurs, and they hadn't done it before.

The mammals did not die out— obviously! They were small and could survive changes in climate better than the dinosaurs.

There were huge volcanic eruptions 65 mya in India that pumped out lava and produced huge dust clouds. These blew all around the Earth and would have blacked out the Sun, leading to darkness and cold.

Whatever happened 65 mya, the whole natural system collapsed. If the plant-eaters died out first, then the predators would have gone too, since they would have had nothing to eat.

# IMPACT!

There is now very strong evidence that Earth was hit by a huge meteorite, about 6 miles (9.7 kilometers) across, 65 mya. The impact threw up huge clouds of dust, blacking out the Sun, and leading to freezing, dark conditions for a year or more.

Meterorite impact

The meteorite hit Earth on the coast of Mexico. A huge crater, 124 miles (200 kilometers) across, has been found, buried beneath younger rocks. The crater was mainly in the sea 65 mya.

When a big meteorite hits Earth, it has enormous impact. It drives a long way into the ground and then turns to vapor. Then, very quickly, there is a huge back blast and millions of tons of rock and dust are thrown back up into the air.

The force of the back blast forms a huge crater.

Meteorite drives into Earth.

Back blast makes crater.

After the dust cloud came a huge fireball of burning gases. Enormous wildfires swept over much of the planet, burning everything in their way.

# RISE OF THE MAMMALS

Mammals were around through the whole age of the dinosaurs, but they were mostly small animals, about the size of a rat. The dinosaurs probably didn't even see them. The mammals kept out of the way and hunted mainly at night.

The first mammals hunted insects and other small creatures while the dinosaurs slept. They could not grow large because the dinosaurs were so successful, nothing could compete with them.

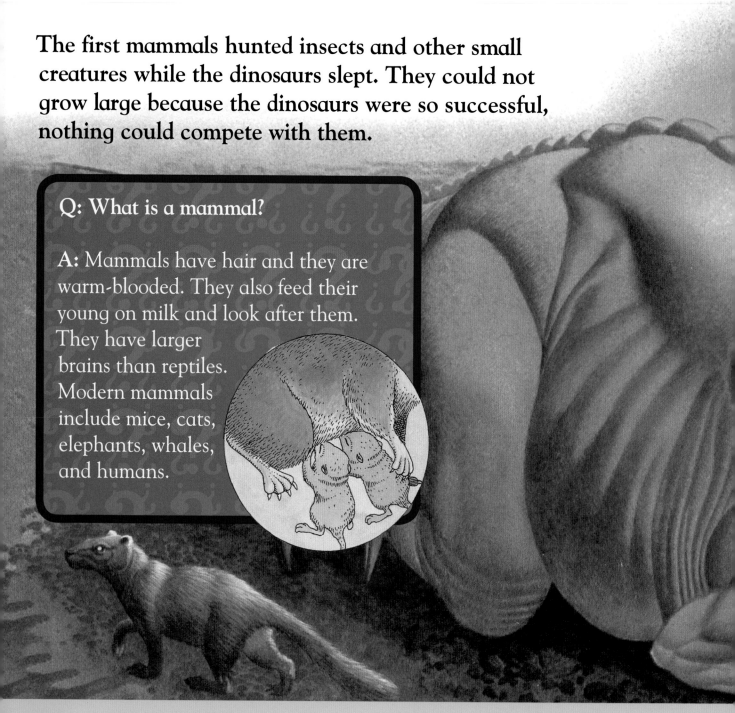

Q: What is a mammal?

A: Mammals have hair and they are warm-blooded. They also feed their young on milk and look after them. They have larger brains than reptiles. Modern mammals include mice, cats, elephants, whales, and humans.

# EARLY MAMMALS

After the dinosaurs disappeared 65 mya, Earth was a strange, empty place. Some birds flew among the trees and small mammals scuttled in and out of the undergrowth. No one then could have predicted that these mammals would rise to rule the world.

## Awesome facts

All modern mammals, from tiny bats to huge whales, first appeared within 10 million years after the dinosaurs had gone.

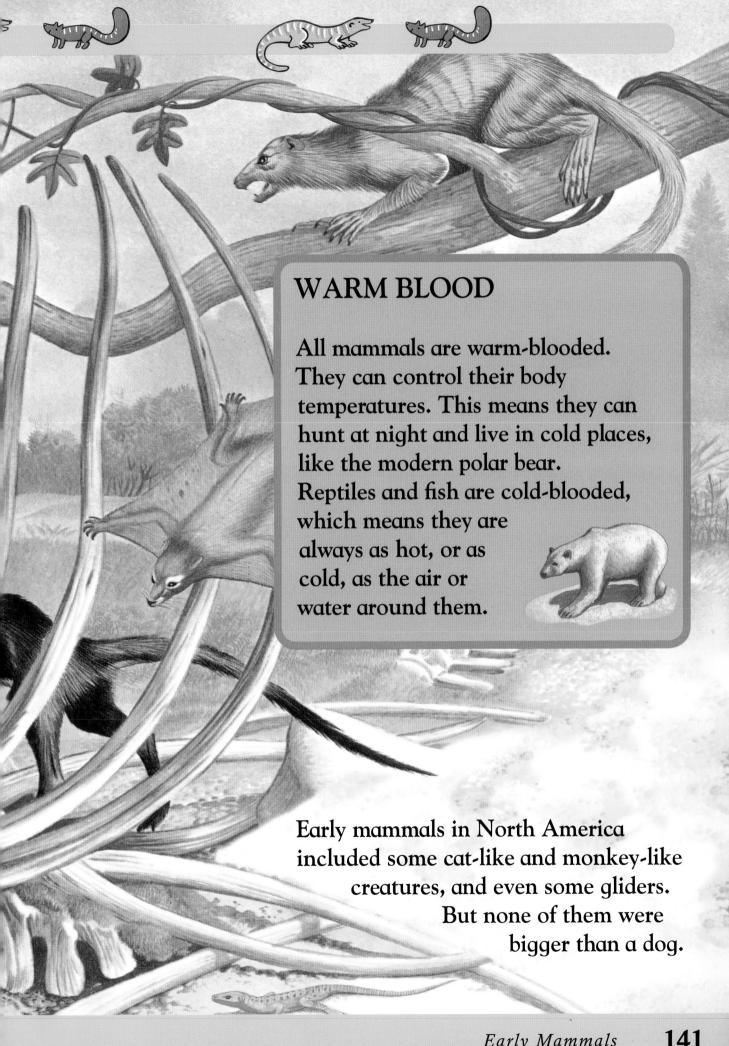

## WARM BLOOD

All mammals are warm-blooded. They can control their body temperatures. This means they can hunt at night and live in cold places, like the modern polar bear. Reptiles and fish are cold-blooded, which means they are always as hot, or as cold, as the air or water around them.

Early mammals in North America included some cat-like and monkey-like creatures, and even some gliders. But none of them were bigger than a dog.

# COMPETITION

By 50 mya, many kinds of mammals had evolved. Some modern groups had appeared, like horses and whales, but mammals did not have it all to themselves. Terror birds ruled the world!

Monkeys, apes, and humans are called "primate. The first primates looked like squirrels, but they had big brains and long tails for balancing as the ate fruit and leaves in the trees.

Q: Where did whales come from?

A: Whales breathe air and feed their young milk, so, although they live in the sea like fish, they are mammals. The first whales lived over 50 mya, and they were like seals. They evolved from big, meat-eating land animals like *Mesonyx*.

*Mesonyx*

*Blue whale*

e top predators 50 million
rs ago were not mammals,
t giant birds. At about
feet (3 meters) tall,
*atryma* was a fearsome
nter and fed on smaller
mmals, including the
cestors of modern
rses. These early
rses were only
out the size of
rrier dog, and
e birds would
ish them in
eir powerful jaws.
*atryma's* head
s about the size of
it of a modern horse.

# MAMMAL EVOLUTION

About 20 mya, there were huge changes in landscapes worldwide. Grass had evolved and huge grasslands spread over the continents. Mammals had to adapt, and grass-eaters became very important.

Early elephants had tusks on top of their mouths (like they do today), below their mouths, or sometimes both above and below.

**Q: What did early horses look like?**

**A:** Horses have always looked like horses, but early horses were very small and they had four toes. Over time, horses became bigger and lost their side toes. So now they have a single toe, known as a "hoof."

Modern horse

Early horse

*Paraceratherium* was a giant rhinoceros with a long neck and no horn. At about 20 feet (6.1 meters) tall, this grass-eater was the biggest land mammal of all time.

Giant armadillos called "*glyptodonts*" were early South American mammals. They had body armor and even a spiky tail club. They looked like ankylosaurs, but were not related.

*Mammal Evolution*     **145**

# DINOSAURS TODAY

Although the dinosaurs themselves all died out 65 million years ago, there are still a lot of their relatives around today, as reptiles and birds. Modern reptiles are a mixed bunch— they do not rule the world as they did in the age of the dinosaurs, but there are still 6,500 species of them around the world.

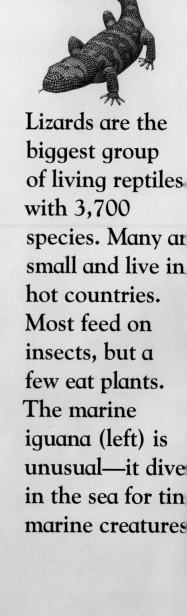

Lizards are the biggest group of living reptiles with 3,700 species. Many are small and live in hot countries. Most feed on insects, but a few eat plants. The marine iguana (left) is unusual—it dives in the sea for tiny marine creatures.

Turtles and tortoises
live both on land and
in the sea. They both have shells
that provide excellent protection
from attack. Tortoises on land move
about slowly, looking for plants or
insects to eat. Marine turtles are
big—some are 6 feet (1.8 meters)
long. They live at sea, but have to
lay their eggs on land.

**Q: Are modern reptiles dinosaurs?**

**A:** No. Dinosaurs' legs extended beneath the animal, while reptile legs extend out to the sides.

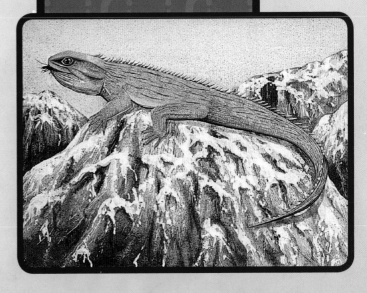

Crocodiles are the closest reptile
relatives of dinosaurs.
Today's crocodiles mainly hunt
underwater, by sneaking up on
animals at the water's edge, then
grabbing them. Crocodiles that
lived with the dinosaurs
(left) could be huge,
and some even
ate dinosaurs.

# LIVING ON

Birds are the closest thing to living dinosaurs. They may not look much like them, but it is now clear that birds arose from small meat-eaters. The first bird, *Archaeopteryx* (see page 132), had a dinosaur skeleton and bird wings and feathers.

A clue to the ancestry of birds can be seen in modern hoatzin chicks. Hoatzins live along river banks in South America. The chicks have claws on their wings, just like *Archaeopteryx*.

## BIRD TEETH

Birds today do not have teeth, but they can still produce teeth in laboratory experiments. This shows that deep in their heritage they once had teeth, but lost them over time.

Modern birds come in all shapes and sizes, from tiny hummingbirds no bigger than a moth, to the giant albatross and condor.
Birds live all over the world, from penguins at the poles to parrots in the tropics.

n ostrich looks very much
ke the ostrich dinosaur,
*truthiomimus*, but they
re not closely related.
Ostrich ancestors could fly,
hen they lost that ability.
Ostriches still have small wings,
but they now only use
them for keeping cool.
Ostriches can run very
fast to catch their prey,
so they don't need to
be able to fly.

*Struthiomimus*

**Q: Do we know everything about dinosaurs?**

**A:** No! Scientists learn new things about dinosaurs every day. Each year, about 20 new species are named, and there are lots more to be found. New studies tell us new things about how dinosaurs lived, and powerful computers allow paleontologists to calculate exactly how dinosaurs walked and ran. All of this means more and more accurate dinosaur models can be made. Life as a paleontologist is never dull!

# GLOSSARY

**Amber**
Fossilized resin from a conifer tree.

**Ammonite**
A prehistoric shellfish with a coiled shell, common in Mesozoic seas.

**Amphibian**
A backboned animal that lives both in water and on land, such as a frog.

**Ancestor**
An historical forerunner of an animal group.

**Ankylosaur**
An armored plant-eating dinosaur, with a covering of bony plates and sometimes a bony knob on the end of its tail.

**Belemnite**
A prehistoric shellfish with a straight, bullet-shaped internal shell, like a modern cuttlefish.

**Ceratopsian**
A plant-eating dinosaur with a bony frill at the back of its neck and one or more horns on its face.

**Cold-blooded**
A cold-blooded animal needs to take its body heat from outside sources, sometimes by basking in the Sun.

**Conifer**
An evergreen tree, such as a pine, with cones and needles.

**Continental drift**
The movement of the continents over time.

**Coprolite**
A fossilized excrement.

**Cretaceous**
The geological period that lasted from 145 to 65 million years ago.

*Cynodont*
A mammal-like reptile similar to the very first mammals.

**Deciduous tree**
A tree that sheds its leaves.

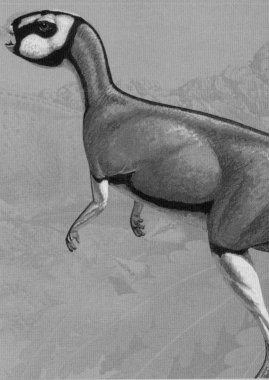

## NA

...ands for Deoxyribonucleic ...id, a chemical inside every ...nt and animal cell, which ...rries the information that ...ntrols the development of ...e body. All species have ...fferent DNA.

## ...uckbill

...n ornithopod dinosaur of the ...te Cretaceous period, with ...duck-like snout. Duckbills ...e sometimes called ...adrosaurs."

## ...volution

...he processes by which ...l plants and animals are ...lieved to have appeared ...llions of years ago, or how ...ey changed over time.

## ...ossil

...he remains of any ancient ...ant or animal, usually ...eserved in rock.

## ...ene

...specific part of the DNA ...hemical, which carries the ...ode for a particular feature ...a plant or animal.

## ...eological

...nything to do with the study ...rocks.

## Hadrosaur

An ornithopod dinosaur of the Late Cretaceous, with a duck-like snout. Hadrosaurs are sometimes called "duckbills."

## Hatchling

A young animal that has just hatched out of the egg.

## Ichthyosaur

A sea reptile common in the Mesozoic period, which had a streamlined body and swimming paddles.

## Jurassic

The geological period that lasted from 205 to 145 million years ago.

## Juvenile

A young animal, older than a baby, but younger than an adult.

## Keratin

The protein that makes up reptile scales, as well as birds' feathers and human hair and nails.

## Limestone

Rock made from lime (calcium carbonate), often created by the shells of ancient animals.

## Mammal

A backboned animal with hair, which feeds its young on milk, such as a cat, a horse, or a human.

## Marginocephalian

A plant-eating dinosaur with armored margins (borders) on the back of its skull, such as a ceratopsian or a pachycephalosaur.

### Nautiloid
A long and pointed prehistoric shellfish.

### Ornithischian
A "bird-hipped" dinosaur, such as an ornithopod, marginocephalian, or thyreophoran.

### Ornithopod
A two-legged plant-eater from the ornithischian group, such as *Iguanodon* and the duckbills.

### Ossified tendon
A muscular attachment that has turned to bone and acts as a strengthening rod.

### Pachycephalosaur
A plant-eating dinosaur with a hugely thickened skull roof.

### Paleontologist
A person who studies fossils.

### Pangaea
An ancient supercontinent that consisted of all the modern continents joined together as one.

### Plesiosaur
A long-necked Mesozoic sea reptile that hunted fish.

### Mesozoic
The geological era that lasted from 250 to 65 million years ago, sometimes known as the "age of dinosaurs."

### Meteorite
A lump of rock from space that hits Earth or any other planet.

### Migration
The movement of animals from one place to another in search of food or breeding grounds.

**iosaur**
short-necked
esozoic sea reptile that
nted other smaller sea
ptiles—a relative of the
esiosaurs.

**redator**
meat-eater—an animal
at hunts others for food.

**ehistoric**
efore history"—describes
ything that is from ancient
nes, such as the dinosaurs.

**rosauropod**
plant-eating dinosaur
th a long neck and tail,
m the Late Triassic or
rly Jurassic periods.

**erosaur**
flying reptile of the
esozoic period, closely
ated to the dinosaurs.

**adioactivity**
ays" of chemical energy
at are given off at fixed
tes. Measuring radioactive
ements in ancient rocks
lows geologists to calculate
e ages of the rocks.

**Raptor**
A hunter—often refers
to dinosaurs like *Deinonychus*
and *Velociraptor*.

**Reptile**
A backboned animal with
scales that lives on land and
lays eggs, such as a dinosaur,
a crocodile, or a lizard.
Ichthyosaurs and plesiosaurs
were marine reptiles.

**Sandstone**
Rock made from grains of
sand cemented together.

**Saurischian**
A "lizard-hipped" dinosaur,
such as a theropod or a
sauropodomorph.

**Sauropod**
A long-necked, long-tailed,
giant plant-eating dinosaur.

## Sauropodomorph
The group name for large, long-necked, plant-eating dinosaurs, such as sauropods and prosauropods.

## Scavenger
A meat-eater that feeds off animals that have died or have been killed by others.

## Skeleton
The framework of bones inside the body of a backboned animal.

## Species
One particular kind of plant or animal, such as *Tyrannosaurus rex*, the panda, or human beings.

## Stegosaur
A plant-eating dinosaur that had bony plates and spines sticking upright along its back and tail.

## Supercontinent
"Big continent," such as Pangaea, which was made up of several continents before they separated.

## Theropod
A meat-eating dinosaur.

## Thyreophoran
An armored dinosaur, such as a stegosaur or an ankylosaur.

## Triassic
The geological period that lasted from 250 to 205 million years ago.

## Vertebra (plural Vertebrae)
Each of the small bones that make up a backbone.

## Warm-blooded
A warm-blooded animal, such as a mammal or a bird, creates heat inside its body from the food it eats.

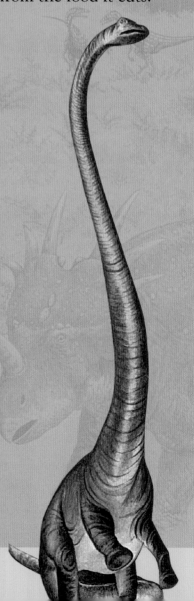

# INDEX

...ertosaurus 9, 27, 43, ...115, 121
...igators 63
...osaurus 29, 30, 31,

...ber 8, 150
...monites 127, 150
...cestors 25, 50, 102, ...3, 143, 150
...kylosaurs 98, 102, ...0, 111, 112, 113, ...4, 115, 116, 117, ...8, 119, 120, 121, ...5, 150, 154
...rognathus 62, 131
...tosaurus 26, 27, 32, ...47, 64, 65, 68
...haeopteryx 28, 34, ...2, 133, 148
...nor 66, 98, 99, 102, ...8, 110, 111, 113, ...5, 116, 117, 118, ...0, 145, 150, 151, ...4

...bies 33, 51, 86, 87, ...91, 93, 114, 128, ...9, 131, 151
...osaurus 107
...yonyx 9, 36, 37, 43
...varisaurus 32
...ak 79, 90
...lemnites 127, 150

birds 10, 17, 34, 38, 39, 63, 83, 87, 124, 131, 133, 140, 142, 143, 146, 148, 151, 152, 154
boneheads 72, 73, 88, 89, 94
bones 9, 12, 13, 17, 23, 26, 37, 38, 40, 41, 49, 51, 57, 58, 60, 61, 63, 66, 72, 74, 80, 81, 86, 104, 105, 111, 116, 117, 120, 149, 151, 152, 153, 154
*Brachiosaurus* 47, 60, 61, 69, 107
brain 23, 24, 100, 138, 142

*Camarasaurus* 49, 69

*Carcharodontosaurus* 41
*Carnotaurus* 8, 118, 119
ceratopsians 72, 88, 89, 92, 93, 94
*Ceratosaurus* 26, 27, 28, 29, 42
*Cetiosaurus* 56, 57, 68
*Chasmosaurus* 93

cold-blooded 25, 63, 102, 103, 141, 150
*Compsognathus* 32, 33, 34, 42, 43
conifers 113
continental drift 11, 150
Cope, Sir Edward 29
coprolites 79, 150
*Corythosaurus* 17, 75, 84, 95
crest 74, 75, 84, 85, 118
Cretaceous 10, 11, 20, 30, 37, 40, 43, 66, 68, 69, 72, 73, 74, 76, 80, 84, 89, 90, 94, 95, 98, 111, 113, 116, 119, 120, 121, 124, 128, 132, 150, 151
crocodiles 36, 56, 57, 124, 147, 153
cynodonts 24, 25, 102, 103, 150

deciduous trees 106, 150
*Deinonychus* 22, 23, 35, 43, 113, 153
*Diatryma* 143
*Dilophosaurus* 28
*Dimorphodon* 131

*Diplodocus* 46, 47, 48, 59, 62, 63, 64, 69
DNA 8, 151
dragonflies 15, 32
*Dryosaurus* 78, 79, 94
duckbills 72, 73, 75, 76, 78, 84, 86, 94, 151, 152

*Edmontonia* 114, 121
eggs 38, 39, 86, 87, 128, 131, 134, 147, 151, 152, 153
*Elasmosaurus* 126
elephants 46, 51, 61, 93, 138, 144
Eoraptor 16
*Euoplocephalus* 8, 118, 119, 121
evolution 14, 144, 151
extinction 69, 134

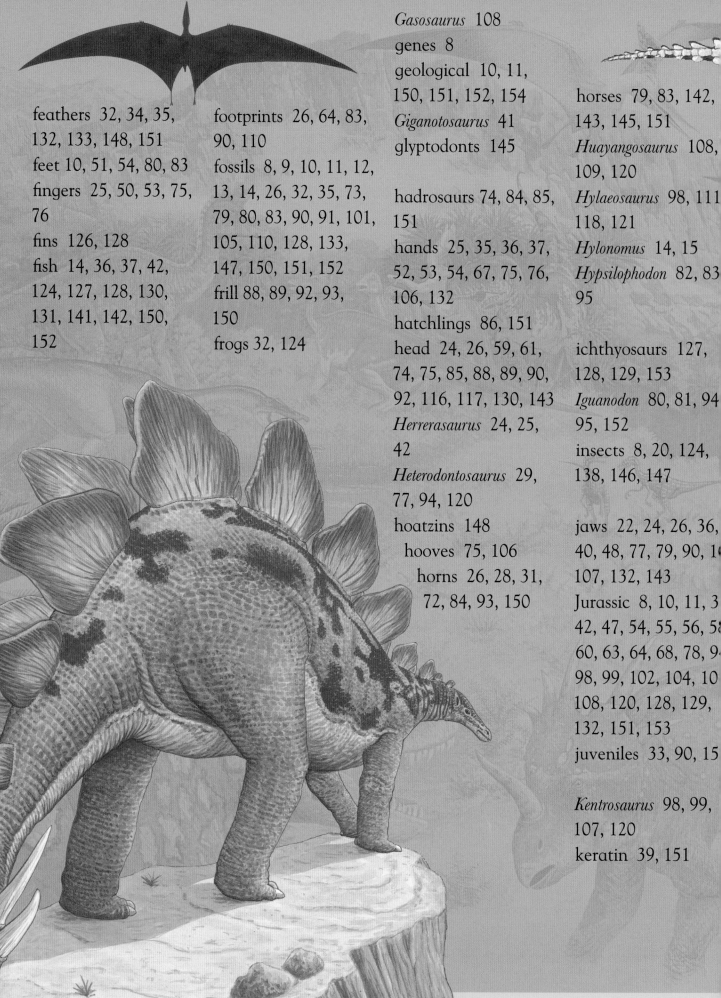

feathers 32, 34, 35, 132, 133, 148, 151

feet 10, 51, 54, 80, 83

fingers 25, 50, 53, 75, 76

fins 126, 128

fish 14, 36, 37, 42, 124, 127, 128, 130, 131, 141, 142, 150, 152

footprints 26, 64, 83, 90, 110

fossils 8, 9, 10, 11, 12, 13, 14, 26, 32, 35, 73, 79, 80, 83, 90, 91, 101, 105, 110, 128, 133, 147, 150, 151, 152

frill 88, 89, 92, 93, 150

frogs 32, 124

Gasosaurus 108

genes 8

geological 10, 11, 150, 151, 152, 154

Giganotosaurus 41

glyptodonts 145

hadrosaurs 74, 84, 85, 151

hands 25, 35, 36, 37, 52, 53, 54, 67, 75, 76, 106, 132

hatchlings 86, 151

head 24, 26, 59, 61, 74, 75, 85, 88, 89, 90, 92, 116, 117, 130, 143

Herrerasaurus 24, 25, 42

Heterodontosaurus 29, 77, 94, 120

hoatzins 148

hooves 75, 106

horns 26, 28, 31, 72, 84, 93, 150

horses 79, 83, 142, 143, 145, 151

Huayangosaurus 108, 109, 120

Hylaeosaurus 98, 111, 118, 121

Hylonomus 14, 15

Hypsilophodon 82, 83, 95

ichthyosaurs 127, 128, 129, 153

Iguanodon 80, 81, 94, 95, 152

insects 8, 20, 124, 138, 146, 147

jaws 22, 24, 26, 36, 40, 48, 77, 79, 90, 1[ ] 107, 132, 143

Jurassic 8, 10, 11, 3[ ] 42, 47, 54, 55, 56, 58 60, 63, 64, 68, 78, 9[ ] 98, 99, 102, 104, 10[ ] 108, 120, 128, 129, 132, 151, 153

juveniles 33, 90, 15[ ]

Kentrosaurus 98, 99, 107, 120

keratin 39, 151

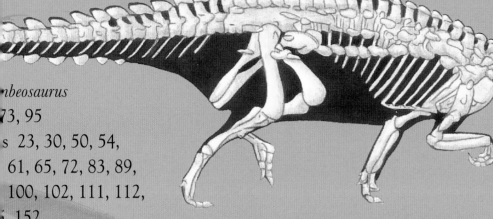

nbeosaurus
73, 95
s 23, 30, 50, 54,
61, 65, 72, 83, 89,
100, 102, 111, 112,
, 152
othosaurus 76, 77, 94
estone 51, 151
leurodon 126, 127
rds 17, 20, 28, 29,
51, 57, 65, 77, 78,
86, 88, 98, 102,
, 127, 130, 146,

iasaura 86, 87, 95
menchisaurus 58
mmals 20, 24, 25,
63, 102, 103, 124,
, 138, 139, 140,
, 142, 143, 144,
, 150, 151, 154

ntell, Gideon 81
ntell, Mary Ann

rginocephalians

rsh, Othniel 29
at-eaters 30, 31,
51, 55, 66, 67, 108,
, 113, 114, 142,
, 153, 154
galosaurus 28, 29
sonyx 142

Mesozoic 10, 11, 42,
124, 126, 130, 150,
151, 152, 153
migration 78, 152
Mososaurus 127
mouth 24, 51, 53,
103, 112, 144

nautiloids 127, 152
neck 46, 47, 49, 56,
58, 59, 60, 61, 69, 89,
93, 126, 144, 150, 152,
153, 154
nests 38, 39, 86, 87,
131

Ornithischia 17, 152
Ornithomimus 20, 43
ornithopods 17, 72,
73, 76, 77, 79, 80, 82,
94, 151, 152
ossified tendon 74,
152

ostrich 149
Oviraptor 38, 39, 43
Owen, Sir Richard
57, 102

pachycephalosaurs
72, 88, 89, 94
paleontologists 8, 13,
34, 39, 40, 57, 80, 86,
102, 105, 149, 152
Pangaea 11, 30, 152,
154
Paraceratherium 144
Parasaurolophus 84, 85,
95
Pentaceratops 93
plant-eaters 25, 32,
46, 47, 78, 89, 152
Plateosaurus 46, 52, 53,
68

plates 66, 98, 99, 100,
101, 109, 110, 116,
117, 150, 154

plesiosaurs 126, 127,
152, 153
pliosaurs 126, 127,
153
Polacanthus 110, 111,
112, 121
predators 25, 27, 66,
67, 76, 83, 93, 108,
113, 116, 118, 119,
135, 143, 153
prehistoric 14, 15,
150, 152, 153
prey 20, 21, 22, 23, 25,
36, 149
primates 142
prosauropods 46, 54,
56, 68, 154
Protoceratops 90, 91, 95
Pteranodon 9, 130, 131
pterosaurs 130, 131,
132

Quetzalcoatlus
130, 131

radioactivity 153
raptors 133, 153
reptiles 14, 24, 25, 28,
29, 38, 63, 102, 103,
126, 127, 128, 130,
138, 141, 146, 147,
150, 151, 152, 153
Rhamphorhynchus 129,
131
rocks 8, 9, 10, 11, 12,
13, 14, 30, 34, 74, 80,
105, 136, 137, 151,
152, 153

Saltasaurus 66, 69
sandstone 51, 153
Saurischia 17, 153
Sauropelta 112, 113,
118, 121
sauropodomorphs 16,
46, 50, 153, 154

sauropods 46, 47, 48,
49, 50, 56, 58, 59, 60,
61, 62, 63, 64, 65, 66,
67, 68, 69, 107, 153
scales 66, 151, 153
scavengers 40, 154
Scelidosaurus 102,
103, 120
shell 9, 13, 38,
100, 147, 150, 151,
152
Sinosauropteryx 34
skeleton 12, 29, 32,
34, 49, 51, 53, 56,
57, 60, 64, 73, 74,
80, 83, 90, 102, 104,
105, 117, 127,
148, 154
skull 24, 26, 31, 36,
53, 88, 90, 116, 117,
127, 151, 152
snakes 124
species 20, 29, 84,
105, 146, 149, 151,
154
spikes 80, 99, 100,
109, 114
spines 37, 60, 98, 99,
108, 109, 114, 115,
116, 117, 154
spinosaurids 36, 37
Stegoceras 72, 73, 88,
95
stegosaurs 98, 99,
100, 106, 107, 108,
109, 110, 120

Stegosaurus 17, 29, 99,
100, 101, 120
Struthiomimus 149
Styracosaurus 9, 73, 89,
92, 95
supercontinent 11, 30,
152, 154

tail 23, 27, 32, 49, 54,
60, 64, 74, 99, 100,
109, 116, 118, 119,
128, 132, 142, 145,
153, 154
Talarurus 116, 117,
118, 121
Tapejara 131
teeth 21, 22, 24, 27,
36, 40, 44, 48, 49, 53,
75, 77, 79, 81, 94, 106,
107, 132, 148
Tenontosaurus 23
Thecodontosaurus
50, 51, 68
theropods 20, 24, 25,
34, 36, 40, 42, 43
Thescelosaurus 12
thyreophorans 98
titanosaurs 66
toes 75, 145
Torosaurus 92
tortoises 147
Triassic 10, 11, 24, 42,
50, 51, 52, 54, 68, 76,
94, 120, 128, 153, 154
Triceratops 93
Troodon 20, 21, 43
Tsintaosaurus 84

Tuojiangosaurus 28, 9
104, 121
turtles 115, 124, 14
tusks 144
Tyrannosaurus rex 16,
20, 21, 25, 41, 42, 4
154

Velociraptor 37
vertebrae 33

warm-blooded 63, 1
whales 138, 140, 14

Yangchuanosaurus 28

Zhiming, Dong 105
Zigong 104, 105